PRODUCTION LINE TO FRONTLINE

CONSOLIDATED
B-24
LIBERATOR

SERIES EDITOR: TONY HOLMES

PRODUCTION LINE TO FRONTLINE • 4

CONSOLIDATED

B-24 LIBERATOR

Michael O'Leary

OSPREY
PUBLISHING

FRONT COVER Finished in Sand camouflage for operations in desert areas (the first three aircraft in this photograph), B-24Ds roll down the San Diego production line as part of Contract 24620 issued on 19 February 1942, which called for 1200 D-models. The line is led by s/n 42-402076

BACK COVER *"MAULIN' MALLARD"* had completed an impressive 115 sorties – recorded on the co-pilot's external armour plate – when it was photographed upon arrival back in the United States at Bradley Field, Connecticut, during May 1945

TITLE PAGE A crewman cleans off the camera port in the nose of *"Ol' Nick"*, an early production B-24D. This variant did not feature the cheek-mounted 0.50-cal gun adopted later in the production run

First published in Great Britain in 2002 by Osprey Publishing
1st Floor Elms Court, Chapel Way, Botley, Oxford, OX2 9LP

© 2002 Osprey Publishing Limited

ISBN 1 84176 023 4

Edited by Tony Holmes
Page design by Tony Truscott
Scale Drawings by Mark Styling
Origination by Grasmere Digital Imaging, Leeds, UK
Printed through Bookbuilderse in Hong Kong

02 03 04 05 06   10 9 8 7 6 5 4 3 2 1

EDITOR'S NOTE
To make this series as authoritative as possible, the Editor would be interested in hearing from any individual who may have relevant photographs, documentation or first-hand experiences relating to the legendary combat aircraft, and their crews, of the various theatres of war. Any material used will be credited to its original source. Please write to Tony Holmes at 10 Prospect Road, Sevenoaks, Kent, TN13 3UA, Great Britain, or by e-mail at: tony.holmes@osprey-jets.freeserve.co.uk

For a catalogue of all Osprey Publishing titles please contact us at:

Osprey Direct UK, PO Box 140, Wellingborough, Northants NN8 2FA, UK
E-mail: **info@ospreydirect.co.uk**

Osprey Direct USA, c/o MBI Publishing, 729 Prospect Ave, PO Box 1, Osceola, WI 54020, USA
E-mail: **info@ospreydirectusa.com**

CONTENTS

INTRODUCTION

WELCOME TO THE FOURTH BOOK in Osprey's *Production Line to Frontline* series. As with the previous volumes, we have attempted to place the design, construction and use of the B-24 Liberator within the period of its greatest use. With the Liberator, this was fairly easy since with the end of World War 2, the United States Army Air Force (USAAF) immediately declared the type obsolete to its post-war doctrine. Accordingly, thousands of Liberators went into storage and most were smelted into aluminium ingots within three years. However, a few were held in the inventory for use as test beds, whilst others were sold into civilian ownership on the military surplus market. Nevertheless, the Liberator quickly became a memory in USAAF history. The US Navy held onto its PB4Y-1s for a longer period, and the last of the significantly different PB4Y-2 Privateers soldiered on into the early 1960s. Unfortunately, little if any thought was given to preserving any of these often highly decorated combat veterans.

The Liberator established numerous records, but perhaps the most important is the way it was churned out of factories across the United States, duly becoming America's most produced World War 2 aircraft, as well as holding the record for the greatest number of bomber aircraft built by anyone at anytime. Yet, somewhat oddly, the Liberator remains greatly overshadowed by the Boeing B-17 Flying Fortress (see *Production Line to Frontline 2*).

When this book was started, I thought that the B-24 was an unattractive aircraft. When the book was finished, I thought the B-24 was a supremely unattractive aircraft! The Flying Fortress was one of those aeroplanes that just looked right, and despite the fact that the Liberator exceeded the Fortress in many performance specifications, the B-17 is the bomber that caught and held the American public's imagination. The B-24 was a more modern aircraft – it was the first production bomber with a nose wheel. The B-24 carried a greater payload than the B-17. The Liberator had a greater range than the Fortress. The B-24 was also faster than the B-17, but none of this mattered – the B-17 was 'the bomber' in America's eyes.

Numerous wartime and post-war movies were based around B-17s, but none were based on B-24s.

Yet men and women toiled to built the Liberator and make sure that combat-ready bombers were flowing to frontline units at an unprecedented rate. In this volume I have attempted to show some of the factors that influenced the design of the B-24, and have attempted to place the aircraft in its time period via vintage aircraft and vintage advertisements that illustrate America's overall national focus to completely defeat the Axis.

As with other aircraft featured in the series, it once again becomes clearly evident just how important the average American woman was to building the Liberator – women that were quickly trained in aeronautical manufacturing techniques and then became so skilled that they often exceeded their male counterparts in wartime production quotas. These women and men came from all across the country – a country still reeling from the effects of the Great Depression – and formed a unique portion of American society, and one that lasted only for the duration of the war. It was during this time period that America went from an agricultural economy to a mighty industrial giant.

Numerous individuals have contributed to this volume, and in particular I would like to thank William T Larkins for his magnificent effort in chronicling the Liberators in storage depots. Thanks also to Milo Peltzer, Harry Gann, Dennis Gibbs and Norm Taylor. Finally, Scott Bloom provided the vintage advertisements from his extensive archives.

Michael O'Leary
Los Angeles, September 2002

CHAPTER 1

BUILDING A BOMBER

ONE WOULD BE HARD-PRESSED to find a more turbulent period than the late 1930s. The industrialised world was still suffering from the effects of the Great Depression, while third world nations were gripped in combat against their colonial rulers. In Spain, a bloody civil war was taking place that pitted Communists against Nazis while serving as a testing ground for a variety of new weapons. In Germany, a dictator had built a huge new military force – at first in secret, but now openly flaunted in public, bringing terror to the various nations on Nazi Germany's borders. In other words, it was an ideal time to build new weapons.

In the idyllic climate of San Diego, California, Consolidated Aircraft Company was going from strength to strength under the dynamic leadership of 36-year-old Maj Reuben Hollis Fleet, who was already a successful businessman when he founded Consolidated in May 1923. Having served six years with the Army's Air Service, Fleet was also an ex-legislator, so his experience, at a relatively young age, was widely varied.

Descended from the Fleets of London, Reuben experienced his first flight in 1914 when he purchased a ride in a primitive flying boat operating from Lake Washington, Seattle. The experience of this first flight would change Fleet's life, and he began flying at every opportunity. Forging ahead in the timber and real estate business, Fleet became the state's youngest legislator, and began to force through various bills promoting aviation. He even circled the state's capitol building in a flying boat.

The young man introduced a bill to fund the National Guard with $250,000 for aviation training – this amount exceeded the funds set aside by Congress for the entire nation! The bill passed through the lower house, but then Fleet let it die when the Army agreed to press Congress to train one guardsman from each state in aviation.

Not surprisingly, Fleet, being a member of the Washington National Guard, was selected for training and shipped off to the Navy's facility at North Island, San Diego, for flight training. Winning his wings on 5 April 1917 (and becoming Military Aviator No 74), Fleet began to undertake various government jobs involved with aviation, including Officer-in-Charge of the Aerial Mail Service on recommendation of Col H H 'Hap' Arnold. Fleet also spent time at McCook Field, Ohio, where he was indoctrinated in the Engineering Division which was doing much to develop and promote aviation after the conclusion of World War 1.

In late 1922 Fleet decided to leave the Air Service and enter into private industry. Turning down excellent offers from Curtiss and Boeing, Fleet originally went to Gallaudet Aircraft Corporation, but quickly moved to the Dayton Wright Company, where a variety of training aircraft were being developed. The company was owned by General Motors, which had limited interest in aviation, and Fleet managed to leverage a deal where he obtained the rights to the trainers as well as the services of chief engineer, Col Virginius Evans Clark. In mid-1923, with leased facilities, Fleet won an Air Service contract to produce the PT-1 trainer, which was a rugged two-seater and a big improvement on the Curtiss Jennys then still in service.

Moving to Buffalo, New York, where he found larger facilities for his Consolidated Aircraft Corporation, Fleet continued building trainers. After Col Clark resigned in 1927, Fleet chose not to replace him, instead establishing various units at Buffalo with an engineer in charge of each unit who reported directly to Fleet. Unit Two was dedicated to flying boats, and was led by Isaac Machlin 'Mac' Laddon, who had joined the company in early 1927. Mac was a creative individual who had started his career with the Engineering Division at McCook, and went on to obtain numerous patents for his designs including the Bendix-Laddon disc wheel and integral brake.

Going through various designs, the company created the XPY-1 Admiral long-range flying boat (which would become the ancestor for the famous PBY Catalina). This was an exceptional design created for missions between California and Hawaii, and Consolidated won a design competition for nine aircraft. However, much to Fleet's chagrin, the production contract was put up for competitive bidding (a common practice at the time) and was won by Martin.

However, Fleet played a clever card and also developed the design as a commercial enterprise – the Commodore – and six were purchased by the fledgling, but dynamic, New York, Rio & Buenos Aires Line (NYRBA). Started by colourful World War 1 flyer Ralph O'Neill, Fleet and James H Rand (Remington Rand) were actually part owners. More Commodores were ordered and the airline became pioneering and profitable, but Juan Trippe of Pan American viewed NYRBA as a thorn in his corporate side and eventually managed to purchase the airline and absorb it, and its aircraft, into Pan Am's growing system.

Fleet went through numerous other adventures and decided that the time was right to build a civilian low-end trainer. Operating under secrecy, Fleet and fellow workers created the design in just 60 hours. First flown in November

1928, the Model 14 Husky Junior soon attracted orders, but the company's directors were very sceptical that the aircraft could make a profit when compared to lucrative military orders.

Infuriated, Fleet personally purchased the rights to the aircraft and, on 22 February 1929, formed Fleet Aircraft Incorporated with the creative Larry Bell as president (Bell would, of course, later go on to establish Bell Aircraft Corporation and build a huge number of military aeroplanes). The aircraft was also named Fleet, and orders soon started pouring in, to the chagrin of Consolidated's directors. Forcing the issue, Fleet Aircraft was sold to Consolidated that August and the company had a successful trainer while Reuben made a tidy profit. Fleet immediately started a cross-country tour with the aircraft to promote sales but, on the last leg, the engine failed and Fleet tried a forced landing but crashed. He was seriously injured and his companion was killed.

From that point on, the company continued growing and Fleet recovered. Fleet Aircraft of Canada was established in 1930 and became very successful, building hundreds of trainers and a variety of other aircraft.

Laddon had created the P2Y Ranger, an updated variant of the Commodore, for the Navy. This was an impressive aircraft immediately ordered by the military. Fleet was becoming disenchanted with the harsh Buffalo weather, and remembering his days during pilot training at balmy San Diego (also home port for the Navy's Pacific Fleet), Reuben travelled to California and struck a deal for a major land lease next to the city's Lindbergh Field. Work continued at Buffalo while the transition was made to the new-built plant in California. This was quite complicated, and 157 rail freight cars were required to move fixtures and supplies. While this was going on, Consolidated received a huge, for the time, order for 60 PBY-1s – the new Catalina. Work stopped at Buffalo on 16 August 1935 and started in San Diego on 3 September – certainly a testimonial to the company's efficiency.

In the new 247,000-square-foot factory, the company was churning out Catalinas, and more orders for this efficient patrol aircraft began to pour in as America attempted to respond to the worsening world situation. Laddon had been moved up to chief engineer and the company was creating a wide variety of designs. In May 1936, the company won a competition for a very large four-engined long-range flying boat – the XPB2Y-1 – and a further expansion to 450,000-square-feet had to be undertaken while 170,000-square-feet of land was paved so that assembly could be undertaken in the open air. This would not have been possible in Buffalo!

With contracts for the initial run of PBYs coming to an end, employment dropped from 3700 to 1200 and the company was looking for new work. Up in Seattle, Boeing was settling in building the new B-17 Flying Fortress bomber and, at the suggestion of high-ranking Air Corps officers, Laddon and

Charles Van Dusen (production manager) travelled to Boeing to undertake discussions about possibly building the Flying Fortress under license.

However, after seeing what Boeing was doing, Laddon left Seattle with the idea that he could build a better and more efficient bombing aircraft for the Air Corps – even though the company had no experience with this type of aircraft.

Before their visit to Seattle, Laddon and Fleet sketched out a design that would become known as the Model 31. The pair wanted to create a flying boat that would be superior to both the Catalina and four-engined PB2Y-1. Using the new Wright R-3350 18-cylinder radial for power, the twin-engined aircraft incorporated a new hull design as well as the new Davis Wing. Even though it had two engines, the Model 31 was an immense aircraft – the airliner version could carry 5400 gallons of fuel for transatlantic trips while hauling 52 passengers. Laddon and Fleet sketched out both civil and military variants.

So enthused with the new aircraft, Fleet decided to proceed with a company-funded prototype without waiting for a Navy order. Without military interference, the company was free to be extremely creative with the Model 31. Fowler flaps were employed along with innovative retractable wing floats that would not harm the efficiency of the Davis Wing. Registered NX21731, the prototype was rolled out in May 1939 and first flown from San Diego Bay on the 5th of that same month by Bill Wheatley and George Newman.

Initial testing showed that the Davis Wing offered a 20 per cent increase in performance, and the pilots' estimated that its top speed would be 250 mph, with a 3500-mile range. Yet despite the Model 31 being greatly superior to both the Catalina and the new Martin PBM Mariner, the Navy, oddly, did not

The massive PB2Y Coronado gave Consolidated vital experience in building large, four-engined aircraft. First flown on 17 December 1937, the basic design required numerous modifications before it was accepted into Navy service

order the aircraft. They cited that it had poor hydrodynamic characteristics at loaded weights, but Fleet reasoned that the Navy passed on the project because it had not been involved in the programme from the beginning.

Laddon decided to use the Model 31's basic wing concept for the new bomber, along with the twin tail arrangement that had been successfully used on that aircraft and the PB2Y. Also, to modernise the design and to enable higher take-off and landing speeds, Laddon designed the aircraft to have tricycle landing gear. Although this was a first for a heavy four-engined bomber, the concept had been tested as retractable tri-cycle beaching gear on the Model 31. Laddon had not been impressed by the Flying Fortress's small bomb-bay, so he created two deep bomb-bays that could carry up to 9000 lbs of weapons. As a concession to the time period, the aircraft was defended with six 0.30-cal Browning hand-held weapons located in the tail, belly, dorsal, waist and nose positions.

Power was to come from Pratt & Whitney R-1830-33 Twin Wasps capable of 1200 horsepower at take-off ratings. They were enclosed in cowlings that were quite similar to those utilised on the Catalina. The Army had given the company wide latitude in creating the new bomber, and this reason, combined with Laddon's ability to incorporate proven aspects of other designs, resulted in rapid progress being made with the new Model 32.

A wooden mock-up was ready for Army inspection on 1 February 1939, and officials liked what they saw. In a typical bit of bureaucratic scheming, the government issued Type Specification C-212 which invited other companies to respond with their own designs. However, the two companies solicited for proposals – Sikorsky and Martin – only had three weeks to respond! Accordingly, on 21 February 1939, the Army recommended that the Model 32 be selected for production and a contract for a single prototype was issued. The new aeroplane was designated XB-24 USAAC s/n 39-556, and a completion date of 30 December 1939 was specified in the contract, which was dated 30 March 1939.

The XB-24 is seen parked on the Lindbergh Field ramp on 26 December 1939 as it is being prepared for its first flight. The short-sleeve weather in San Diego during December is obvious – one of Reuben Fleet's primary reasons for moving from Buffalo, New York. Finished in gleaming natural metal, the prototype bomber features just basic Army Air Corps markings. The XB-24 was many steps away from being an operational bomber suitable for combat over Occupied Europe

As any student of modern history knows, the world situation was going from bad to worse during this period, and while work was proceeding on the prototype, more orders were forthcoming. Seven YB-24s were contracted in April and 38 B-24As were added in August of the same year.

Pulling out all stops to get the prototype airworthy by the specified contract time, wing and fuselage mating took place on 29 October. By December the aircraft was on the ramp for final finishing and engine and systems tests. On 29 December, history was made as the XB-24 gracefully lifted off from Lindbergh Field for a successful 17-minute test flight. Its pilots were Bill Wheatley and George Newman, while Jack Kline and Bob Keith served as flight engineers. Little did these men realise that more than 19,000 B-24s would follow them into the sky to become the largest production American military warplane, as well as being the most numerous bomber of any nation at any time.

Reuben Fleet would later record in November 1941;

'The story of B-24 production revolves around design, construction and the placing into production of the huge new building recently completed at San Diego, which was constructed on the principle that the shortest distance between one finished bomber and the next is a straight line. Raw materials flow into one end of this mile-long defence plant and completed sub-assemblies issue from the other. From there all sub-assemblies travel over a road to the final assembly line which is mechanised to approach true mass production methods. At the end of the mechanised assembly line, the B-24s go into the yard area for final installation of internal fittings, engine and propeller adjustments and testing etc., prior to flight testing and final delivery to the Army Ferry Command'.

Little did Fleet know that this was just the beginning of the Liberator story. Let us take a moment and examine the structure of the B-24 and how it was built. The following applies to the J-model but the same basic techniques were applied to all B-24s.

FUSELAGE

The fuselage was a semi-monocoque shell consisting of smooth skin reinforced with Z-type 24ST Alclad rolled stiffeners or stringers and transverse bulkheads and belt frames. The longitudinal stringers were generally spaced at about six-inch intervals with greater concentrations where required for extra strength. Longerons were used only to carry loads around openings at bomb-bays, access doors and other points where the skin-stringer combination was broken.

Belt frames to maintain fuselage shape were 0.040 24ST Alclad lipped channel, notched to pass over stringers and spaced about 1.5 ft apart.

In the bomb-bays, where belt frames and longitudinal stringers were interrupted, in the lower half of the fuselage, vertical stiffeners were spaced about seven inches apart to avoid

passing stringers around or over bomb-bay door tracks. Side longerons were channel shaped, five inches wide and two inches deep at their widest part in the bomb-bays, tapering out six or eight feet in both directions.

Skin-stringer-bulkhead-belt frame structural design was used because strength was dispersed rather than concentrated in a few critical members – a distinct advantage in any assembly subject to combat damage.

By building the fuselage around the wing, juncture weight was saved through elimination of heavy fittings and bolts at the attachment points, and fuselage torsional stiffness was improved. This method joined the wing and fuselage by means of a continuous riveted and bolted attachment around the periphery of the box structure of the wing, formed by the upper and lower surfaces and the front and rear spars.

At the ends of the bomb-bays were bulkheads, and these were connected longitudinally to a partial bulkhead in the centre between the two bays by a beam which also formed the catwalk. The aft end bulkhead was a plate girder type built up of rolled sections and flat sheet. The upper part of the front bulkhead was a truss, whilst the lower portion was flat sheet. The partial bulkhead between the two bays extended upward only to the wing in order to provide lateral support for the catwalk.

This photograph gives an excellent idea of the scope of Liberator production at the Douglas plant in Tulsa, Oklahoma. Note the hoisting straps around each unit so that they could be slung over to the moving production line when required

The catwalk through the bomb-bays served as a longeron, and provided for transverse and longitudinal loads from the bomb racks. It consisted of two U-shaped channels forming the sides, a corrugated Alclad top serving for the walk, and a smooth Alclad bottom forming part of the outside skin of the fuselage. Diaphragms of pressed sheet, spaced about two feet apart, maintained the cross-section of the catwalk. The catwalk ended aft at a curved box beam, which transmitted loads to two longerons around the ball turret opening. These tapered out four feet beyond the turret opening. Forward, The catwalk tapered out ahead of the forward bomb-bay. Around the nose wheel well, loads were passed through auxiliary longerons.

The nose wheel gear attached at four points. The two upper attachments were to the floor truss of the radio operator's compartment, the truss passing loads from the fuselage sides. Two lower attachments were to the main bulkhead of the pilots' compartment, a plate girder built up of rolled sections and flat sheet transmitting loads to the fuselage shell.

The vertical supports of the rear bomb racks took the form of welded steel tube trusses, which were in turn welded to gusset plates riveted to the rear spar of the wing, while forward

A Liberator is painted at Ford's Willow Run plant. The B-24 could be completely camouflaged in Olive Drab and Neutral Gray by a skilled spray crew in just half an hour. Each of the painters wears respirators to protect against the effects of fumes. Also note how leading edges, engines and Plexiglas areas were covered in masking paper. The paint went on glossy but would dry to a dull finish

racks tied to the lower surfaces of the wing by bolted fittings which passed loads to the wing internal structure. Bomb loads – because of this means of supporting the racks – were actually carried by the wing, rather than to the wing by means of the fuselage. For load purposes, the wing attached to the fuselage through bolting and riveting of channel type bulkheads to the front and rear spars of the wing.

The bomb-bay doors were flexible and made up of corrugated section 24ST Alclad spot-welded and riveted to an outer Alclad skin. To open, they slid up on the outside of the fuselage by means of rollers attached to the ends of the corrugations and running in curved tracks.

The bombardier's compartment was merely a continuation of the fuselage nose section. It was a standard monocoque construction of flat sheet supported by stringers and three bulkheads built of formed U-channels of Alclad and 24ST sheet. Ahead of the bombardier's position, the fuselage supported a tub-like structure in which the forward turret was mounted. Its

Minus engines, accessories and armament, each Liberator comprised approximately 30,000 components which, once production began reaching higher numbers, required around 140,000 man-hours (womanhours, in this case) to turn into a complete bomber

supporting structure was carried on two short and heavy deep beams of 24ST Alclad, bolted to the foremost fuselage station bulkhead by heavy aluminium alloy forgings.

The pilots' enclosure was approximately midway between the front of the fuselage and the leading edge of the wing, and was faired into the main portion of the fuselage.

The flight deck, immediately aft of the pilots' position, had a floor slightly lower than the pilots' floor. It carried drag loads from the main landing gear back to the wing and also supported radio equipment and a radio operator.

Emergency exits were provided in the top of the fuselage above the bombardier and pilot positions, and in the bottom of the fuselage aft of the waist gun compartment for tail and waist gunners. The bombardier could also leave by way of the nose wheel door, and pilots and upper gunner could exit through the forward bomb-bay. Waist and tail gunners could also use the waist gun windows.

WING

Design of the B-24 wing was based on a geometrically similar airfoil used with considerable success on the Consolidated Model 31 flying boat. Ease of production was one of the main considerations in selecting this wing design.

The wing envelope was established by connecting corresponding percentage ordinates of the construction root and construction tip sections. Construction tip and root sections were normal to a chord plane. Each left and right chord plane was set at an angle of three degrees 26 minutes to the horizontal, and the chord section on the plane of symmetry was established by intersections of the percentage point connecting lines. The tip was faired from the construction envelope in conventional manner.

A centre section and two outer panels comprised the main units of the wing and were mated by flush, tension-bolted splices. The spar locations were widely spaced to provide maximum room for fuel cells of sufficient capacity to insure the greater range specified by the USAAF, and also to provide clearance for main landing gear wheels.

The centre section had a span of 55 ft and its structure included two auxiliary spars of plate girder type, built up of heavy, rolled angles and flat sheet riveted to two of the main wing bulkheads to support the landing gear. Both main and auxiliary spars were Wagner type with Z-section vertical stiffeners spaced four to six-inches apart, and rolled angle flanges. To eliminate joggles, the flanges were placed back-to-back on the web against the face of the paired angles. Stiffeners were placed on the web surface opposite the flanges so that the components could be fitted together without the loss of structural efficiency.

Bending loads were carried primarily by the upper and lower surface plate-stringer combinations. There were five

uppersurface skin sections or panels on each side of the centre-line. The upper skin at the root was 0.125 24ST Alclad for the forward 60 per cent of the interspar distance, and 0.091 24ST Alclad for the aft 40 per cent of the interspar distance. These skins extended spanwise 147-inches to the end of the main fuel cell region. The remaining skins on the uppersurface of the centre section were divided into three strips. The forward strip was 0.114, the centre strip 0.102 and the aft strip 0.091 24ST Alclad. The gauge reductions were made to save weight when strength requirements were reduced.

Rolled hat-section stringers of approximately similar gauges were used for skin stiffening. Skin and hat splices occurred at the bulkheads 147 inches from the centreline, and also at the centreline. Forged flange strap fittings and splice plates connected both hat sections and skins. Outboard splice plates were buried, causing the splices to be flush. At the outer panel-to-centre section splice, the hat sections were connected to an inverted flange splice angle by U-forgings riveted to the sides of the hats.

The lower surface plating of the centre panel was stiffened by 1.5-inch drawn Z-sections. The plating and stringers were tapered from even distribution at the splice to bands approximately ten inches wide at the front and rear spars adjacent to the

By 1944, women had really made their presence felt in American aviation manufacturing. This photograph of a Liberator wing being completed features no less than 11 'Rosies' busily at work with sealant

wheel well. The bands were parallel to the main spars, and the plating became continuous at the outboard end of the fuel tank. Material was concentrated by reinforcing sheets which reached a maximum thickness of approximately $3/8$ths of an inch at the wheel well. Spar flanges were joggled to accept the reinforcing sheets, and Z-stringers were spliced by fittings similar to those used for the hats at the main tank bulkheads. Stringers were connected to the wing splice attaching angles by forged T-fittings. Rivets on the uppersurface of the interspar area were machine countersunk. When the required diameter was $3/16$ths of an inch or less, brazier-head rivets were used on the lower surface. All larger rivets were also machine countersunk.

Centre section interspar bulkheads were of three types – Wagner beam, truss and pressed sheet – depending on what loads they carried, type of load and whether access through them was required. There were 27 of them, 13 on each side and one at the centre. The Wagner beam web was flat Alclad sheet and rolled angle flanges set back-to-back with the web on one side and stiffeners on the other. Trusses were Warren type with rolled channel chord members and interconnecting diagonal rolled channels.

The main wing fittings included two hoist fittings which could be used in lifting the entire aircraft in weight-empty condition. They were attached to the bulkhead at the wing centreline.

Landing gear fittings were simple forged flanged bosses, riveted to the auxiliary spars, as well as Wagner type with a web of flat Alclad sheet and rolled angle flanges set back-to-back, the web on one side and stiffeners on the other.

Upper engine mount fitting forgings were bolted and riveted directly to the uppersurface of the front spar, while lower engine mount fittings were carried on a welded tubular sub-structure.

Each outer panel of the wing comprised an interspar structure with a removable leading edge and wing tip, as well as a trailing edge structure forward of and over the flap. The spars were at ten and 66.2 per cent of the chord, and their design was similar to that of the centre sections spars. Interspar ribs were pressed aluminium alloy, and plate-stringer combinations completed the bending box.

The uppersurface employed hat sections at the inboard end, and these spliced into 1.5-inch Z-stringers which in turned spliced down to one-inch stringers and terminated at the base of the wing tip. The lower surface plates-stringer combination was similar, except for the fact that hat sections were not used, 1.5 and one-inch Zs being used for stiffeners. During assembly operations, the wing skins were applied to the uppersurface first. Front and rear strips were then attached to the lower surfaces, and the closure was completed by attaching a centre strip provided with hand holes. New assembly procedures made it possible to attach plate-stringer surfaces as units.

The ailerons were of typical torque-boxed pressed-rib construction, fabric-covered. A two-horn gearbox control system was originally used in connection with these surfaces, but this was discontinued in favour of a single-horn push-pull-tube bellcrank system. Trimming tabs were provided on both ailerons.

Most of the rolled sections in the Liberator wing were stretched approximately 3.5 per cent to the RT condition, and since few extrusions were used, Consolidated was able to control section output simply by using sheet stock. Although rolled sections were not as dimensionally accurate as extrusions, little trouble was experienced in constructing the wings because of flexibility of the fundamental design.

The Fowler flaps had an area of approximately 144-square-feet and a movement downward of 40-degrees. The individual flap was supported by roller carriages, which engaged five tracks, four of which were attached to the centre section and the fifth attached to the outer panel. Tracks were steel I-beams bolted to a tubular planar truss. Clevises at the forward ends of the tubular truss attached to lugs which protruded through the spar at the spar flanges and attached to bulkhead chord members. Flap controls comprised a cable system actuated by a hydraulic cylinder energised by pressure from the main hydraulic system.

Engine mounts attached to the front spar of the inner section of the wing, these being made of welded 4130 com steel tubing. They were of two-bay type, $45^3/8$th inches long. Attachment was at four points, by tension bolts, the upper two being to the spar and the lower two to after-mounts which projected downward from the lower surface of the wing, because of the thin wing design.

Space in the forward bay, behind the steel firewall was occupied by an oil tank, and the oil cooler, on the right side, and intercooler on the left side. The aft bay provided space for the turbosupercharger and its regulator.

The entire assembly – mount, engine, cowling and accessories – was assembled as a removable unit which, while standardised, was not interchangeable in other than the intended location.

Each Pratt & Whitney Liberator engine had its own completely independent oil system consisting of a self-sealing reservoir of 42-gallon capacity located within and attached by brackets to the engine mount; a temperature regulator located behind the engine and within the mount; an oil dilution system; and drains, piping, controls and oil separator.

Each powerplant was attached by eight flexible shock mounts. Engines numbers 1 and 2 drove the instrument system vacuum pumps and number 3 drove the main hydraulic system hydro-pressure pump.

Each powerplant was enclosed from the nose ring to the wing by Alclad cowling, except around the exhaust system, where stainless steel was used.

Before the United States entered the war, many young men, most just out of high school, were eager to escape towns across America that were still in the grips of the Great Depression, and the aviation industry was hiring at full force. Realising that the southern California worker pool was being drained by the numerous aircraft factories, Reuben Fleet cast his hiring net across the country, and was able to acquire an eager and skilled work force. These two young men are putting the final touches on a portion of Liberator cowling

Mounted in its special jig, a Liberator ring cowl receives work at the Vultee plant in Downey, California. Vultee was just one of the many B-24 subcontractors

THE DAVIS WING

The 110-ft wing of the Liberator was its most distinctive feature. Developed by David R Davis for the Consolidated Model 31 flying boat, the wing was a radical departure from airfoils then in use. During tests of the wing at the California Institute of Technology's wind tunnel in Pasadena, California, engineers were surprised by the wing's performance. Compared to the conventional NACA Number 230 airfoil, the Davis Wing showed a decrease in drag of 20 per cent, which meant a substantial increase in range, speed and lift – just the right combination for the new heavy bomber.

Efficiency of a wing depends upon its size, shape and, particularly, airfoil. Various combinations of these are used to develop the most efficient wing for a particular purpose. The Davis Wing had just the right amount of camber, together with a peak pressure point in the right position, to form an ideal wing for a fast, heavy bomber. From the fuselage the Davis Wing was a straight tapered, high-aspect-ratio wing to the tip, giving it an efficient, symmetrical appearance.

Although the basic wing form was already in existence in 1939, when work commenced on the B-24 it had to be radically modified internally to carry four engines and the retractable landing gear. Power-operated Fowler flaps were another feature which increased the wing efficiency. On the trailing edge of the wing, these sections slid out to increase wing area, thereby giving the aeroplane more lift when needed.

BELOW A newly-built B-24 climbs towards its high-altitude environment, showing the high-lift Davis Wing to advantage. David Davis signed a contract on 10 February 1938 with Consolidated whereby he would be a consultant on the design. He would work a minimum of eight days a month for a six-month contract, being paid $200 per month. Secretive about his design, Davis would at first only deal with Reuben Fleet. The wing would be tested at Cal Tech, in Pasadena, and if it worked Davis would get $2500 for the prototype and 0.5 per cent of the sale price on each B-24 built

LIBERATOR WING DATA

Airfoil Section designation
Root - CVAC 22 per cent
Tip - CVAC 9.3 per cent

Wing Area - 1048 sq ft

Span - 110 ft

Root Chord - 14 ft

Tip Chord - 5 ft 2^{13}/$_{32}$ in

Thickness at Root - 22 per cent

Thickness at Tip - 9.3 per cent

Incidence - 3 deg

Dihedral on Upper 30 per cent
Chord Line - 1 deg 30 min

Sweepback (leading edge) - 3 deg 30 min

Trailing Edge Sweep Forward -
5 deg 38 min

Twist - None

Spar Location, Front -
10 per cent chord

Spar Location, Rear -
66.2 per cent chord

Aspect Ratio - 11.55

Mean Aerodynamic Chord, Length -
123.72 in

Location Relative to LE LW
(Chord-Horizontal) - 17.04 in aft

Root Chord, Vertical - 16.6 in above

TAIL SURFACES

The horizontal tail surfaces of the original design had NACA section No 0015 and contained 192 square feet. Span was 26 ft and maximum chord 7 ft 8³/₁₆th inches. Distance from the design gross weight centre of gravity, assumed at 25 per cent MAC, to the one-third maximum chord point was 33.40 ft, which was approximately 3.5 times MAC. Stabiliser area, including elevator balance, was 140.5-square-feet. Its normal setting relative to the longitudinal axis was 2.5-degrees.

The elevator had an area of 67.1 square feet, with 51.5 square feet aft of the hinge line. Angular movement was 30 degrees up and 20 degrees down. The elevator was aerody-namically balanced and all span-wise elements were statically balanced about the hinge line. Tabs in the trailing edge had an area of 4.95 square feet and were controlled by an irreversible mechanism.

Vertical tail surfaces had NACA section No 0007, with a fin area of 123 square feet and rudder area of 48.8 square feet. Rudders were aerodynamically balanced and fully balanced

This worker is linsetting an Alclad panel into a Liberator vertical tail at Vultee's Downey factory. Also noteworthy is how the leading edge was created with riveted rectangles of Alclad in order to avoid expensive compound curves

statically. Spanwise elements were statically balanced about the hinge line. Tabs had a total area of 3.1 square feet, and were equipped with irreversible controls. Rudder angular movement was ten-degrees right and left of centre.

All tail assembly control surfaces were of aluminium torque box and rib construction, covered with fabric. The stabiliser, constructed as a separate assembly, had a smooth sheet metal skin and was attached to the fuselage with only four fittings to facilitate replacement. The entire tail assembly was mounted just enough forward of the tail gunner's compartment so that the trailing edge did not obscure the gunner's vision.

PROPELLERS

The B-24's propellers were the Hamilton Standard Hydromatic three-bladed constant speed type, with quick feathering features. Clearances were 37 inches to the ground and 23.5 inches to the fuselage. Normal distance to the plane of each propeller disk was 74.6 inches at the centreline of the inboard engine. Controls were electrical and convenient to both pilot and co-pilot. Feathering pump oil was obtained from the main oil tank.

Consolidated designed jigs which were constructed from standard pipe and clamp fittings so that production changes could be made with minimal cost and effort

Propeller anti-icing was achieved with two electrically driven pumps installed below a 21-gallon tank located above the wing centre section, between the life raft doors. One pump supplied pressure for both inboard propeller anti-icer rings and the other for the outboard propellers.

Anti-icing systems for pilots' and bombardier's windshield exteriors were connected directly to the same tank. The de-icing and defrosting of window interiors was achieved by heat exchangers and flexible defroster tubing adjustable for direction against the windows.

LANDING GEAR

The Liberator's landing gear was tricycle type, with a fore and aft wheel base of 16 ft and a main gear width of 26 ft 7.5-inches. In addition to the main gear and the nose wheel, a retractable tail skid was provided which, while not strong enough for full tail landing loads, could withstand the load of rocking after landing. The skid was supported by an Alclad sheet box structure built into the lower aft end of the fuselage, below the aft gun position, and was extended and retracted hydraulically.

The main gear wheels were Air Corps Type 111, made of aluminium or magnesium alloy castings, requiring 56-inch by 16-ply tyres. The nose wheel boasted a 36-inch by ten-ply tyre.

Hydro-pneumatic struts were used on the main and nose gears, with the main gear retracting outward and upward into wells in the undersurface of the centre wings, and the nose wheel retracting upward and slightly aft into a well just forward of the pilots' cockpit floor. The nose wheel was held in the up position by a latch, and the fairing door over the well was actuated by the gear mechanism.

The main gear assembly was supported by two false, or auxiliary, spars located just outboard of the inboard engine cowling, between the front and rear spars. They were of plate girder type construction, built from heavy rolled angles and flat sheet that was in turn riveted to two of the main wing bulkheads. Both gears were equipped with emergency release and retraction mechanisms. Brakes were duplex expander tube type.

FUEL TANKS

Two integral fuel tanks, each extending 147 inches from the wing centreline, were installed in the first Liberator wing. Sealing was accomplished by placing 1/32-inch synthetic rubber gaskets in the tank seams. Little trouble was experienced with this type of construction, which had been previously developed and proved in PBY Catalinas, but military requirements made it necessary to replace the integral fuel tanks with self-sealing cells. Later, auxiliary cells were added in the area outboard from the wheel wells to the first outer panel bulkhead, providing still great range.

No basic design change was required to effect the fuel tank changes. A larger access door on the underside, removable members in two bulkheads adjacent to the ends of the tank region, and small access doors through which to reach fuel cell manifolds were provided constituted the only wing changes required. Space for the additional tanks existed in the original wing and was now merely being utilised.

There were 18 self-sealing fuel cells installed in the wing, nine on each side of the centreline. The 12 inboard cells made up the main fuel cell system with a capacity of 2343 gallons, and six outboard cells comprised the two auxiliary systems with a capacity of 450 gallons, giving a wing tank capacity of 2793 gallons. Two additional cells with a combined capacity of 790 gallons could be installed in the forward bomb-bay.

The 18 cells comprising the normal or wing system were interconnected by flexible self-sealing manifolds to make six units of three cells each. Main system manifold connections were accessible through access doors in the lower surface of the wing. Auxiliary system manifold connections were reached from the inboard side of inboard nacelles. Main system units of three cells with interconnecting manifolds had a fuel booster pump located under the final cell of the unit, a shut-off selector valve, fuel strainer and engine-driven pump.

Normally, fuel from one main unit was delivered independently to one engine (engine number 1 from system number 1). Fuel was transferred from the auxiliary to the main cells by the fuel transfer system. Connection of the auxiliary cells to the engines was through the crossfeed system.

Main fuel cells in the wing centre section were held in place by their fit into the compartment. Where the cell did not completely occupy the full fore and aft depth, spacers were installed between the cell and front spar. Canvas curtains snapped into place between the sides of the cells and the rib members.

The centre section compartment was provided with a drain on each side of the centreline to discharge overboard any fuel which might leak from the cells. Flanges of these drains were located immediately aft of the two inboard booster pumps and were fitted with shut-off valves and overboard discharge lines.

The booster pump gland drained empty into these lines. The drain outlets led through a bulkhead on each side of the catwalk and extended below the skin. The wing compartment vent lines were located on each side of the centreline of the inboard nacelles and passed through the centre of the wing spar and out through the wing lower surface aft of the numbers 2 and 3 nacelles

ANTI-ICING SYSTEM

The leading edges of the airfoils were originally designed for boot-type de-icers, but later models of the Liberator featured Consolidated's new exhaust-heat anti-icing system. This made it necessary to provide ducts and double skins for conducting heated air to the leading edge surfaces. Edge strips, screwed to a ledge at the spar flange, made it possible to attach the leading edges by means of self-locking nuts in gang channels.

Air heated by exhaust gases was piped through the leading edge and the other parts of the Liberator – pilots', radio operator's, tail gunner's and bombardier's compartments, and the upper turret position. Other crew positions relied on electrically heated clothing for protection.

The system consisted of a heat exchanger in the exhaust stack just ahead of the turbosupercharger, four in all, through which outside air was passed before flowing through ducts to the wing, empennage and fuselage compartments. Ducting took the form of aluminium sheet tubing covered with sheet asbestos, and averaged five-inches in diameter.

OTHER SYSTEMS

For offensive action, the Liberator could carry four to 22 bombs in its two bays, and additional bombs in external racks attached to the undersurface of the inboard wings. Later versions of the bomber carried an average of ten 0.50-cal guns aimed and fired

An Emerson A-15 turret in the nose of a Ford-built B-24H. This view shows the 'bicycle chains' in the turret – one of the prime items removed from Liberators for resale when they were being scrapped by the thousands following the end of the war. Note the protective covering to the optical glass bomb aiming panel. Ford developed the design and modification to add the Emerson unit to the nose of the Liberator, and although it weighed 190 lbs more, pilots stated that the Emerson unit did not cause as much air disturbance as the Consolidated turret

Numerous Liberators were retained by the factories or by the Army Air Force for testing. Based at Orlando, Florida, this B-24D received a wild disruptive camouflage which designers hoped would confuse the aim of enemy fighter pilots. It didn't

from side openings and in pairs in four power-operated turrets mounted in the nose, top fuselage, belly and tail. The remaining two weapons were flexibly mounted so that they could be manually aimed and fired from the side waist enclosure in the aft portion of the fuselage. Armour plate protected areas around all crewmembers and vital equipment.

The main hydraulic system of the Liberator operated the wing flaps, bomb-bay doors, wheel brakes and landing gear. Rear gunner's turret was hydraulically powered by a separate system mounted on the right side of the fuselage adjacent to the tail turret. The system was a combination of the better features of the direct pressure and open centre systems, and was termed an open centre pressure and return unit.

The B-24's electrical system had three main sources of energy – batteries, generators and a 2-kW auxiliary power unit located on the left side of the fuselage just ahead of the bomb-bay and below the flight deck. The units connected to a common distribution system which covered the entire aircraft. The DC to AC inverters supplied energy to special equipment requiring alternating current.

Radio, interphone and directional radio equipment aboard the Liberator derived power from the 24-volt DC supply of the main power system. The interphone consisted of an amplifier, dynamotor and jack box, with one throat microphone and microphone-amplifying equipment for each crew station. Each throat microphone was equipped with a switch cord or a push-to-talk switch.

The command radio consisted of two transmitters and three receivers, and was mounted above the wing centre section just aft of the life rafts. A modulator unit, dynamotor modulator unit and dynamotor were mounted aft of the compass receiver on the rack for the radar equipment. A liaison radio included a transmitter located on the flight deck, under the radio operator's table, and a receiver on the table. The radio compass was located over the wing centre section on the right side and the maker beacon was located in the bomb-bay.

The capacity of the oxygen system, originally provided by five fixed-position bottles in the upper aft section of the outboard engine mounts, was increased to 26 bottles of 350-psi type, located at strategic points. The pressure scale, translated in terms of altitude, was controlled by the user and maintained at a setting 5000 ft higher than the indicated altitude.

FLIGHT TESTING

Flight testing of the XB-24 showed a shortfall in performance (top speed of 273 mph instead of the specification's 311 mph) and the Army wanted changes. As a direct result of combat reports emanating from Europe and the Far East, the prototype would have to be altered. Accordingly, Pratt & Whitney R-1830-41 radials were installed and these were equipped with turbosuperchargers which allowed for more performance at greater heights. Also, it had been illustrated in battles over Europe and the Far East that self-sealing fuel tanks and added armour plate were absolutely mandatory for any bomber – no matter how high or fast it flew. The XB-24 was duly modified to meet Army demands, and the re-equipped aircraft was redesignated XB-24B and, oddly, given the new serial 39-680. The XB-24B returned to the air on 1 February 1940.

Going back to April 1939, a desperate French Purchasing Commission had visited Consolidated and ordered an export variation of the bomber – the LB-30MF (Mission Francise). The LB stood for Land Bomber, and the French wanted 175 examples in short ordered. However, the French were soon overrun by the German *Blitzkrieg* in May-June 1940, and Hitler's next target – Britain – decided to take over part of the French order.

On 17 June 1940, Britain requested 135 of the aircraft as LB-30 Liberators. Contrary to some sources, the name Liberator had already been assigned by Consolidated and was not a British creation. It must be remembered that the Air Corps was not particularly fond of names at that time, preferring the military designations instead. The British, already having felt

the Nazi sting, wanted the bomber to be equipped with power turrets, self-sealing tanks, armour etc.

Since their need was so obvious, a deal was struck on 9 November 1940 that saw the Royal Air Force (RAF) receive 26 of the first B-24s that were going to be delivered to the Air Corps. Six YB-24s went to the RAF as LB-30As, and since these aircraft were not really combat ready, they were assigned to the transatlantic ferry route and performed that difficult mission in a most heroic manner. These were followed by 20 B-24s which were designated Liberator Is (for remaining details on British Liberator deliveries and production see chapter three).

The Army accepted the seventh YB-24 – which had been modified with armour and self-sealing tanks – in May 1941. This was followed mid-year by nine B-24As which were not combat capable, so they were utilised for training. Two of these machines were later employed as transports for the important Harriman Mission to Moscow in September 1941. Two more were equipped for a clandestine reconnaissance mission to see what the Japanese were up to on Truk and other islands but this never took place because of the 7 December 1941 surprise attack on Pearl Harbor. One of these aircraft was caught on the ramp by strafing Zeros and burned out to become the first American Liberator loss of World War 2.

Reflecting the mood of a stunned nation following the Pearl Harbor raid, Reuben Fleet made the following statement to the press on 19 December 1941;

The second LB-30A Liberator I (which started out life as a YB-24), AM259 was photographed at New York prior to its transatlantic flight to Britain. Due to Britain's urgent need for aircraft, this aeroplane was obtained directly from the first Army Air Corps order for the type. A lack of self-sealing fuel tanks and armour protection rendered the type unsuitable for combat over Europe, so the RAF, in conjunction with British Overseas Airways Corporation crews, used the aircraft to perform vital transatlantic flights ferrying diplomats, VIPs and ferry crews picking up combat aeroplanes in America. Note that although the Liberator has been completely camouflaged, the outer surfaces of the propeller blades have been left in a highly polished finish

'America's bomber programme and the spirit which will beat Hitler and the Japs is exemplified by the tremendous production programme which has been conducted by Consolidated Aircraft Corporation, and which is now proceeding at an ever-growing rate. The expansion of production and facilities by Consolidated is probably an all-time record for any aircraft plant, but it typifies what has been happening throughout the aircraft industry. With several million square feet of factory under roof and in production in the San Diego area alone, as we enter 1942, not to mention an additional vast area used year-round for final assembly work, the Consolidated production expansion seems almost magical in the smoothness and simplicity with which it has been achieved.'

From December 1941 through February 1942, the Army would receive nine B-24Cs. The B-24C was a 'stepping stone' aircraft that would lead the way to Liberator mass production. It incorporated changes from the combat front and was equipped with a Martin power turret in the upper forward fuselage and a Consolidated power turret with twin 0.50-cals fitted in the tail. A 'tunnel gun' was installed in the belly of the rear fuselage, but it would soon be found that this was extremely inadequate. The Cs were fitted with Pratt & Whitney R-1830-41 turbosupercharged engines, and this led to a revision of the cowling which would give production Liberators an oval cowl with two large air intakes that supplied the turbosupercharger and its intercooler. Consolidated dubbed the Cs 'production breakdown aircraft', and they would not be used in combat but would be utilised for flight and groundcrew training.

The B-24D was the first mass-production Liberator and the Air Corps began receiving its first examples in late January 1942, the urgency of the war feeding a speed-up in production. The Ds mounted Pratt & Whitney R-1830-43 engines fitted with 11 ft 7 in diameter Hamilton Standard propellers. A single 0.50-cal gun was installed in a ball socket in the nose, but the

Of the seven YB-24s contracted, the Air Corps would receive only one example – s/n 40-702. Seen on a test flight, the various fuselage windows fitted to the earlier variants are clearly visible. Delivered in May 1941, the aircraft was fitted with self-sealing tanks, armour and fittings for 0.50-cal machines guns instead of the 0.30-cal weapons specified in the original requirement. This unique variant was utilised for training, and was the first Liberator finished in Olive Drab and Neutral Gray camouflage. The short nose of the very early versions is clearly evident in this view

Finished in Sand camouflage for operations in desert areas (the first three aircraft in the photograph only), B-24Ds roll down the San Diego production line as part of Contract 24620, issued on 19 February 1942, which called for 1200 D-models. The line is led by s/n 42-402076. Ahead of government orders (and also ahead of the priorities jam), Consolidated ordered over $6,000,000 worth of machine tools and equipment, then set about quadrupling the size of its San Diego plant. However, no amount of forward planning produces results unless it is backed up with hard cash, machines, and men. Consolidated was very fortunate in the field of financing its expansion effort, for at the very start of its building programme, the company was bolstered by a strong financial position and an excellent record, making initial financing a matter of routine. Advance cash payments on the large foreign orders became available to bridge the gap to government allocations for factory construction and equipment

inadequate tunnel gun was replaced (starting with the 77th B-24D, 41-11587) with a remote control Bendix belly turret with two 0.50-cal weapons. This was the same turret utilised on early B-17Es, and it was also totally inadequate.

Resting on his knees, the gunner had to aim the turret through a periscope that protruded from the aircraft's belly. Hard to use, the position could also cause vertigo and nausea in

An interesting view of Liberator noses and armament. The aircraft on the left has the greenhouse nose with no armament, the middle bomber has the greenhouse with three 0.50-cal hand-held weapons and the B-24 on the right has the power turret with 'twin fifties'. The turrets were a huge improvement over the hand-held weapons, which were ineffective in opposing head-on attacks

the gunner. After building 287 Ds with the turret, production was revised to eliminate the mounting and plate over its opening. The tunnel gun was reintroduced until B-24D 42-41164 which saw the installation of the much superior Sperry ball turret (built by Briggs). This turret could retract into the fuselage for landing and take-off (the belly clearance on the Liberator was quite low) and, once lowered, could rotate 360 degrees while the twin 0.50-cal weapons could elevate from zero through 90 degrees. The addition of the Sperry ball turret was a major plus in defending the Liberator. Also, as production continued, two more 0.50-cals were added in socket mounts to the nose, but this was still inadequate in protecting the aircraft from determined head-on attacks.

The B-24D would also see the introduction of the Liberator Production Pool, and after only five months of San Diego production, Ds started rolling off the line in May 1942 at Consolidated's new facility in Fort Worth, Texas (oddly, and showing the many, many non-sensical variations in Liberator production, none of he 303 Fort Worth Ds would have the ball turret). In July, the Douglas facility at Tulsa, Oklahoma, began deliveries of B-24Ds assembled from components, but only ten Ds would be assembled. Final B-24D assembly would stand at 2696 machines, with San Diego contributing 2381 bombers. Five factories would eventually be building Liberators at an unprecedented rate.

The B-24E was essentially a D-model with some minor changes – R-1830-65 radials with improved propeller blades were installed on the majority of machines (however, in

RIGHT Sea-Search Liberators pour from the Fort Worth factory in this staged photograph to illustrate American mass-production capabilities. The undersurfaces were painted Insignia White (shade 46) while the uppersurfaces were Dark Olive Drab

ABOVE Another view of the San Diego production line, this time with B-24Ds in Sea-Search camouflage rolling down the line (s/n 42-40823 in the lead). Initially, Fleet thought that finding adequate personnel in the San Diego area (rather sparsely populated until the start of the war) would be a problem. The nearest metropolitan centre was Los Angeles, some 125 miles to the north, and the heavy hiring programmes of aircraft companies in that area made it impracticable to obtain the bulk of Consolidated employees there. The company duly organised its employment programme so as to bring in people from other parts of the country, thus allowing Consolidated to swell its payroll by more than 1500 per cent in less than 24 months, and without competing with other west coast aircraft plants

LIBERATOR PRODUCTION POOL

As with the Boeing B-17 Flying Fortress, it soon became obvious that many more production facilities were needed to build the number of Liberators required by the military. Consolidated soon opened a second massive factory at Fort Worth, Texas (CF), Douglas was contracted to build B-24s at its Tulsa, Oklahoma, plant (DT) and North American Aviation began churning out Liberators at its factory near Dallas, Texas (NT). America's pioneer proponent of mass production, the Ford Motor Company, soon got into the swing of Liberator production too.

In early 1941, Ford design personnel visited the San Diego factory, and a plan was started whereby Ford would start making B-24s at an entirely new plant at Willow Run, Michigan (FO). The people at Ford got busy and quantified the Liberator into 20,000 separate functions, breaking it down in much the same way they would have done with a car.

BELOW Early Ford-built B-24E s/n 42-7076 is trailed by a North American B-25B Mitchell. Many of the early Liberators off the various production lines were assigned to stateside training bases to instruct flight crews and ground personnel on the new bomber (*Harold W Kulick*)

As part of the license agreement to build the bomber, Ford erected its new factory on a 65-acre site, and it cost $1,000,000 per acre to construct the immense half-mile long, quarter-mile wide building. The agreement was that Ford would build 'knock-down' Liberator kits to supply to the other license builders for completion (Ford would build a stunning 1893 knock-downs). The company would also build complete bombers.

Skilled in the mass production of cars, Ford employees were not skilled aviation production workers, so the company redrew 30,000 B-24 drawings to make them easier to interpret – not a bad idea, and one from which Ford would benefit.

Learning from the early lack of communication with the B-17 production pool, coordination between the different Liberator factories was a priority, and the Army insisted that an overall coordinating committee be established. This was done, and during 1942-43, the committee functioned in total, but then went on to deal with individual problem cases as required, giving an idea of the efficiency that had been achieved.

Henry Ford himself proved to be a problem for the committee. A strong proponent of the Nazis during the 1930s, he refused to hire women, permit smoking or allow unions into his factory. There were

constant battles with unions and strikes, causing extreme ill-will on the part of the military personnel that showed up to accept new aircraft.

The government began to exert increased pressure on Ford who, at age 79, started to give in, and Willow Run began to operate more efficiently and soon became a model of wartime production. In short order, Ford would be rolling out a Liberator every 63 minutes by mid-1944. The company would go on to construct 6792 complete aircraft, and supply 1893 knock-downs. The following summary gives an idea of the scope of B-24 manufacturing:

MODEL	CO	CF	FO	DT	NT
XB-24	1				
LB-30A	6				
Liberator I	20				
YB-24	1				
B-24A	9				
Liberator II	140				
B-24C	9				
B-24D	2415	303		10	
B-24E		144	490	167	
B-24G					430
B-24H		738	1780	582	
B-24J	2792	1558	1587	205	536
B-24L	417		1250		
B-24M	916		1677		
XB-24N			1		
YB-24N			7		
C-87		280			
C-87A		6			
AT-22		5			
PB4Y-2	740				
RY-3	34				
R2Y	1				
TOTALS	7645	3034	6792	964	966

GRAND TOTAL: 19,401

another maddening deviation, the Douglas-built Es had -43s). The E-model also saw Ford Motor Company at Willow Run, Michigan, enter the B-24 production fray. The many constant production changes on the various Liberator lines infuriated that maven of American mass-production, Henry Ford. He duly had the aircraft slightly redesigned to accommodate his concept of the moving production line, where the B-24 flowed down a line with various equipment being added at specific stages. Only 801 Es would be built, with Ford contributing 490, Tulsa, 167 and Fort Worth 144.

The follow on B-24G was still basically the same as the D-model, and was constructed exclusively at the North American Aviation facility at Dallas, Texas (which was also grinding out Mustangs and Texans). The Gs initially started out with R-1830-43 engines, but with the introduction of the G-10-NT, power

upgraded to the R-1830-65 while the Sperry ball turret was also added. The first 25 Gs retained the greenhouse nose, but with the 25th example a power turret was added. North American would crank out 430 G-model Liberators.

The B-24H picked up on many of the features added to the B-24G line, with Emerson power turrets being featured in the nose and tail positions. Also, the H-model saw the inclusion of improved waist gunner positions, along with numerous other minor changes. Initially, it was planned to use R-1830-65s on the H production run, but -43s were installed on the H-DT, H-1-CF and H-1-FO runs. Tulsa would build 582 Hs. Fort Worth 738 and Willow Run 1780 for a total of 3100 B-24Hs. Notably, numerous Hs were later upgraded to J configuration, but these were not redesignated.

The next production run of the B-24 would also be the most numerous Liberator built. The B-24J was similar to the B-24H, and production was instigated at San Diego during August 1943. The J had a new bombsight and autopilot, while the nose and tail turrets were Consolidated units instead of the Emersons. For the J series, power was standardised on the R-1830-65, but the dozens of different block designations had modifications too numerous to list. All five plants built B-24Js – totalling 6678 – with Tulsa building 205, Dallas 536, Fort Worth 1558, Willow Run 1587 and San Diego 2792.

The B-24L was similar to the J but had a pair of hand-held 0.50-cal weapons in a Consolidated tail position – once again another seemingly needless, time consuming, change to the production line. The first B-24Ls were delivered in mid-1944, with Ford building 1250 and San Diego 417 for a total of 1667.

The last major production variant of the Liberator was the B-24M. Similar to the L, the aircraft had a lightweight Motor Products tail turret with 'twin fifties' – a complete change from

This Liberator is fitted with a Consolidated A-6 nose turret and finished in Sea-Search camouflage. One of the most effective anti-submarine aircraft of the war, Liberators served with distinction with the USAAF's Anti-submarine Command, which was activated on 15 October 1942. Initially equipped with obsolete aircraft such as the Douglas B-18 Bolo, the command soon replaced these with Liberators. Anti-submarine Command existed for only ten months, yet it operated from four continents, and during its service the number of U-boats destroyed by air attacks increased ten fold. Following the command's stand-down many of its Liberators were transferred to the Navy

Transition. Gleaming in its natural metal finish, B-24J USAAF s/n 44-40850 is framed by the outer wing and engine of a camouflaged aircraft. As the war in Europe progressed, the need for camouflage became less and less, and by deleting the painting process, man-hours were saved and overall weight decreased. Photographed on the San Diego ramp, natural metal and camouflaged bombers can also be seen being serviced behind these aircraft under camouflage netting

ABOVE Gear coming up after eating up most of the runway at Holman Field in St Paul, Minnesota, a Liberator thunders aloft after receiving work at the Northwest Airlines modification centre. Since production on the B-24 was running at such high rates, the addition of the latest equipment or modifications could not be incorporated without greatly interrupting the flow from the lines. Liberator modifications centres were therefore set up o handle such additions at Consolidated's Fort Worth facility, Oklahoma City Air Material Center, Tucson Modification Center in Arizona, Birmingham Modification Center in Alabama, Northwest Airlines in St Paul, Martin in Omaha and the Hawaiian Air Depot. Some 3000+ B-24s went through the Northwest facilities at Holman Field and Vandalia, Ohio, these being major centres that employed over 5000 workers. Northwest converted many B-24s into F-7 photo-reconnaissance aircraft. Today, the hangars are still in existence at Holman, although they are currently home to the fleet of Gulfstream business jets operated by the giant 3M corporation

ABOVE The flight test crew of San Diego-built B-24M USAAF s/n 44-42276 take their new Liberator down low for a spot of sightseeing along the California coast. The M was the last production variant of the B-24, and would feature a greatly improved canopy for the pilots (this aircraft does not have it, however, for the improvement would come only on Block 20 aircraft – another maddening difference that plagued the numerous Block variants of the B-24) and a lightweight Consolidated A-6B tail turret. Once again, in yet another confusing Block change, some 41 L-models were inexplicably fitted with the Consolidated M-6 turret – these aircraft were built in the B-24L-165 Block (*Martin and Kelman*)

the hand-held weapons in the L! San Diego delivered 916 Ls and Willow Run 1677 for a total of 2593 aircraft. With the end of the war near, and the cancelling of contracts, there is little doubt that the Liberator was overbuilt. Indeed, many airframes were flown directly from the factories to storage facilities for resale or scrapping.

However, the massive numbers of B-24s constructed guaranteed that the Americans, and their Allies, had a massive bombing force that the Axis could not hope to stop.

ABOVE Well-dressed Consolidated employees are seen on and around the last Liberator to roll off the San Diego production line. Note the PB4Y-2 Privateer in the background

THE UNGAINLY N

The Liberator was certainly not an attractive aircraft. Admittedly, beauty is in the eye of the beholder, but the ugliest variant had to be the B-24N. Engineers had been concerned about the Liberator's stability, so an attempt to improve this shortcoming was undertaken. Using a B-24D, Consolidated removed the twin tails and replaced them with a modified unit from a Douglas B-23 Dragon. Given the unofficial designation B-24ST (single tail), some test flying was undertaken, but the modification was not particularly satisfactory.

As detailed elsewhere in this book, the US Navy was the last user of the Liberator in the USA. Finished overall yellow, PB4Y-1 BuNo 32309 was utilised for testing early missiles and is seen carrying KU3N-1 anti-shipping weapons. Note the post-war national insignia (*Norm Taylor*)

ABOVE The last one. After scrapping thousands of combat-veteran Liberators, the USAF retained this final B-24 – EZB-24M USAAF s/n 44-51228 – for a wide variety of testing experiments. Its last use was for ice research with the Wright Aeronautical Development Center, and it remained in the inventory until 1953. Upon its retirement, instead of being cut up, 44-51228 went to Lackland AFB, Texas, where it served as a gate guard for decades. With the help of the Ford Motor Company, the aircraft was transferred to the American Air Museum in Britain in 1999, where it has been the subject of a detailed static restoration. In September 2002, former President George Bush rededicated the museum, with the B-24 occupying an important position to signify its contribution to the war effort in the ETO

A new vertical tail was fabricated and, along with a horizontal stabiliser from a Douglas C-54 Skymaster, this unit was added to a later production B-24D which took to the air on 9 September 1943 as the XB-24K.

Flown to Eglin AAFB in Florida, the XB-24K was extensively test flown and pilots found that stability and handling improved, while the new tail also gave the tail gunner a much better field of fire. The test force recommended that all future

An inflight view of the XB-24N. Along with improved nose and tail turrets, the N-model had upgraded waist gun positions

An Emerson 128 ball turret in a test rig. The Emerson unit was an improvement on earlier turrets, and also greatly aided B-24N performance since it streamlined the aircraft's nose and got rid of most of the buffeting caused by earlier turrets. Note that the gunner is fully enclosed inside the turret, almost in a fetal position

Liberators be built with single tails. Also, the highly-modified nose and Emerson 128 ball turret offered a much smoother airflow, and test pilots praised the installation compared to the buffeting caused by the earlier blunt nose turrets.

Accordingly, contracts were issued for massive numbers of the new variant, which would be designated the B-24N. Ford was assigned to build a stunning 5176 B-24Ns, and XB-24N-FO s/n 44-48753 was delivered in November 1944. Fitted with Pratt & Whitney R-1830-75 radials and the new nose and tail turrets, with its massive single vertical tail, the new variant was a singularly ugly machine. The X was followed by seven YB-24Ns for operational testing. Along with the Emerson nose turret, these aircraft had A-6D tail turrets which were built by Southern Aircraft Corporation, being lightened variants of the earlier SAC and Motor Products turrets.

Officials planned to replace the L with the N, but at this late stage of the war there seemed to be little thought devoted to the future role of the Liberator. At Boeing, and other plants, B-29s were rolling off the production line, and the Allied juggernaut was rolling over the Germans on its way to Berlin. Despite the N offering some improvements over the B-24J/M, it was not in the same performance league as the Superfortress. By this point, the Liberator had been overbuilt, but officialdom showed no sign of slowing production

Apparently some thought was given to sending a few of the YB-24Ns to a combat front in Asia but this never happened, and after VJ-Day the aircraft were quickly scrapped, thus ending Consolidated's hopes of producing an improved Liberator.

If the N-model had entered series production, somewhere along the line the waist guns would have been eliminated in favour of this twin 0.50-cal barbette, which would have been aimed and fired by the gunner in the waist position

CHAPTER 2 HAULERS

Fully camouflaged LB-30A AM259 carries the large civil registration G-AGCD on the rear fuselage, underlined in red, white and blue, while being operated by BOAC for the RAF. The first six Liberators off of the Consolidated production line were completed as LB-30As for the RAF. Although delivered in combat configuration, the aircraft lacked self-sealing tanks, thus rendering them unacceptable for combat over Europe. The six Liberators were therefore handed over to a grateful Ferry Command, who stripped out all armament and installed a few creature comforts such as cabin heat and oxygen for passengers

JUST AS SOME of the LB-30 Liberators were converted into transports, it became obvious to the military that a specific cargo/passenger variant might be highly desirable. In early 1942, crash-landed B-24D USAAF s/n 42-40355 was retrieved from its resting spot in the Arizona desert, disassembled and hauled back to San Diego, where Mac Laddon and his team made a full-scale effort to turn it into a transport that could be mass produced. The fuselage was gutted and 25 seats were added, while windows were mounted in the fuselage. The compartment for the navigator was relocated behind the flight deck and the top turret was replaced with an astrodome.

To enhance the carriage of outsize cargo, a double cargo door was installed in the left side of the fuselage. The door opened to six by six feet, which enabled the aircraft to carry a wide variety of cargo. The tail turret was also eliminated, and its position covered with a fairing. Once finished, the aircraft was painted Olive Drab and Neutral Gray, with the name *Pinnochio* applied to the modified nose. Designated XC-87, the aircraft made its first flight on 24 August 1944.

Flown to Bolling Field, Washington DC, *Pinnochio* was tested by none other than Gen Hap Arnold, who liked the aircraft and put in motion a contract that would result in 73 C-87s being built with the name Liberator Express. The

prototype was flown to Fort Worth for study, and B-24Ds on the line were duly converted into C-87s.

The initial order was followed by another contract for 111 transports, 24 of which would be supplied to the British as Liberator C VIIIs. Oddly, the C-87s did not use block numbers to denote changes to airframe or systems, despite there being six different variants of the basic Liberator Express. The USAAF started receiving its transports on 2 September 1942, and deliveries were completed on 10 August 1944. Production reached a peak in March 1944 when 21 transports were delivered. The US Navy received five C-87s with the designation RY-2.

A follow-on version was developed in the form of the C-87A, but this would be a transport with a difference since it was intended to haul VIPs, boasting just 16 seats which could be converted into five berths. Because of the different seating arrangement, the fuselage windows were also deleted. Six C-87As were ordered and three went to the Navy as RY-1s. The USAAF aircraft were named *Gulliver I, II* and *III*. C-87A USAAF s/n 41-24159 was assigned to President Franklin Roosevelt and renamed *Guess Where II*. This aircraft effectively became the first Air Force One, although it was certainly never called that.

Numerous Liberators were converted in the field to transports. Some had the designation CB-24 while others

ABOVE The USAAF procured six C-87As which were configured as 16-passenger VIP transports. Three of these went to the Navy as RY-1s, and RY-1 BuNo 67787 was photographed with its national insignia partially painted over after the end of the war, probably indicating a surplus sale. The jack in the tail kept the fuselage from dropping on its tail

BELOW An LB-30 sits alongside a de Havilland Mosquito at the de Havilland facility outside Toronto, Canada. The hard-working LB-30s did an exceptional job hauling ferry crews back and forth across the Atlantic, allowing vital Lend-Lease aircraft to be delivered by air rather than as deck cargo on slow and vulnerable ships (*A W Gifford*)

retained their original bomber designations, which leads to much confusion for historians. Consolidated proposed a C-87B, which would be armed with five 0.50-cal Brownings, but this variant was not built. At least five C-87s were modified to AT-22 trainers for flight engineers. This designation was later changed to TB-24D, and the fuselage was modified to carry a crew of five and thirteen instructors and pupils. A small number of B-24s were also field modified into basic C-87 configuration, and Ford even modified a Liberator as the Ford Utility Transport, but this aircraft differed in many details from the C-87.

Not only was the hauling of cargo and personnel to battle-fronts of extreme importance, but with America's widening war against the Axis, the transport of aviation fuel began to assume more and more importance. Ships could not get fuel into remote areas often surrounded by the enemy, so the lifting of fuel by air became a reality. During 1943, Ford modified a B-24E into the XC-109 flying fuel tanker, with the addition of eight fuel tanks – one in the nose, two in the forward bomb-bay, two in the aft bomb-bay and three in the rear fuselage. This allowed for the carriage of well over 2000 additional US gallons of fuel. It also made the aircraft into a fairly dangerous beast.

Ford converted 199 B-24L/J airframes into C-109s while Martin undertook a further nine conversions, although these utilised flexible tanks instead of the light alloy tanks in the other aircraft. Initially, the aircraft were fitted with an on-board

C-87 USAAF s/n 44-52987 was the last of its type to be built, and the aircraft was photographed on a pre-delivery test flight near Fort Worth, Texas

ABOVE The RAF's Liberator II was the first variant of the basic design to sport the three-foot nose 'stretch' demanded by Reuben Fleet to improve the aircraft's appearance. Liberator II AL592 was converted to C II cargo/passenger configuration and operated by British Overseas Airways Corporation (BOAC) for the RAF from August 1942 until war's end – note the company's distinctive Speedbird insignia on the nose. As with many Liberator cargo conversions, there was a great deal of individuality in each modification, as can be seen by the fitment of circular windows instead of the more standard rectangular units. The nose cone of this aircraft was hinged to allow for the loading and unloading of cargo through the nose (*Gordon S Williams*)

ABOVE During World War 2, BOAC performed some legendary flights with their Liberators on behalf of the RAF. Originally, these aircraft were painted up in full Consolidated-applied camouflage, with large civilian registrations underlined in red, white and blue. Also, crews wore their airline uniforms and were covered by the rules of the Geneva Convention. When, during January 1945, BOAC handed back surviving Liberators to the RAF, a decision was made to purchase eight machines for civilian conversion. AM920 became G-AHYB, and was photographed with its cargo door open. Note the RC-108 blind-landing antenna mounted on the canopy frame. These aircraft gave BOAC an important heavy-lift capability (*Gordon S Williams*)

APU (Auxiliary Power Unit) to aid in pumping the fuel out of the aircraft. However, the fuselage was so full of fumes that this became a very dangerous procedure, and external pumping systems were adopted. The Liberator could also carry a portable A-6 refuelling unit to more remote locations.

The C-109s were mainly operated by Air Transport Command (ATC), and they went into action in the China-

Burma-India theatre, but there were several accidents on airfields above 6000 ft. The ATC instituted a new training programme for pilots that had to be completed before they were allowed to fly their first C-109 mission. This improved safety somewhat, but with fully loaded tanks the C-109 was an unstable beast, and it was decided after initial operations to leave a tank in the forward fuselage empty in an attempt to improve performance and stability.

C-109s were shuttled back and forth over the Hump, bringing in vital fuel supplies to support B-29 Superfortress operations out of China. Due to hazardous weather conditions, the India-China Wing of ATC was able to fly just 45 tons of supplies into China during the first ten days of 1943, causing hardships for the Fourteenth Air Force. Supply was so crucial that ATC established a C-87 route from Patterson Field, Ohio, to China on 12 September 1943. The round-trip flight covered 28,000 miles and took a dozen days to complete. By January 1944 ATC was losing three crewmen for each thousand tons of supplies reaching China, and the command would eventually lose over 1000 crewmen. Initially, it was thought that a massive fleet of 2000 C-109s would be required to supply the bombers, but with the success of the island-hopping war in the Pacific, this plan was dropped when the Marianas Islands were taken over for B-29 bases, as these could be supplied by US Navy oilers.

ATC operated a mixed bag of LB-30s, C-87s, C-109s and B-24s between March 1943 and October 1947. It originally had 71 aircraft in its inventory, and its force strength peaked in January 1945 with 308 Liberator variants. By February 1946 there was just one Liberator variant flying with the ATC.

Due to the USAAF's burgeoning need for aerial supply, ATC recruited many pilots and crews from US airlines due to their

Liberator II AL578 was one of 140 such aircraft ordered directly by the RAF. These aircraft had provisions for Boulton Paul turrets fitted with four 0.303-in machine guns, and although one machine had the turrets installed at San Diego, the remainder had their defensive equipment fitted after arrival in Britain. Numerous airframes were converted into transports, including AL578, which also retains its waist hatches. Named *Marco Polo*, this aircraft was occasionally used by Prime Minister Winston Churchill. It was photographed at Montreal, Canada, in September 1944. Following wartime service with No 45 Group and No 113 Wing, the veteran Liberator was struck off charge on 30 May 1946 and sold for scrap (Robert O'Dell)

ABOVE During World War 2, BOAC operated Liberators (again note the Speedbird on the nose) across the globe in conjunction with the war effort. These aircraft were mainly used for carrying important cargo and passengers over the Atlantic. BOAC also flew Liberators on the North Atlantic Return Ferry Service, flying crews to America to pick up Lend-Lease aircraft. Regular flights to Moscow were also undertaken by the airline from October 1942 through to March 1943. AL507 is seen here having the covers removed from its flying surfaces before a flight from an unidentified, snow-laden, airfield. This particular aircraft was one of eight Liberators purchased by BOAC when the fleet was returned to RAF control in January 1945. Converted into a civilian freighter, AL507 duly became G-AHYC and remained in service into the late 1940s

expertise in long-distance flying. For these men, the acronym ATC quickly became known as the 'Army of Trapped Civilians'. American Airlines, United, Pan American and Consairways (a contraction of Consolidated Airways, operated by civilian crews) also undertook cargo flights for ATC.

Although the cargo and fuel variants of the Liberator performed a heroic mission, they were not particularly liked by the crews – especially the civilian airline crews, who considered the type very dangerous due to their constant fuel leaks. With the end of the war, most surviving aircraft were sent to the storage yards, and few tears were shed.

ABOVE This 'short nose' RB-24A-CO USAAF s/n 40-2377 was typical of the many Liberators converted 'in-the-field' from bombers into transports. Since these early variants really had no effective combat role, they became vital cargo haulers during the early days of the war. The aircraft was photographed on 1 August 1945 (*Harold G Martin*)

ABOVE With the end of the war, a few cargo Liberators were fitted out for full civilian use, and these aircraft provided a vital transport link until newer and more suitable aircraft became available. One such aircraft was Liberator C II AL552, which was flown by Scottish Airways as G-AHZR. Photographed over Scotland in 1946, the aircraft was one of three Liberators utilised during the Berlin Airlift. G-AHZR was modified as a fuel hauler and flew 489.21 hours (148 missions) during the vital airlift. In that time, the vintage Liberator lifted 1182.5 tons of fuel. The aircraft then went on to become SX-DAB in Sweden and finally F-BEDS in France (*Norm Taylor*)

ABOVE Proudly wearing a large Air Transport Command motif on its rear fuselage, this Liberator C II (LB-30) was one of 26 such aircraft retained by the USAAF from RAF orders so that the British could take delivery of 26 early-build B-24s. Modified to passenger/cargo configuration, AL594 served throughout the war, and was photographed in fairly pristine condition awaiting an uncertain future at Kingman, Arizona, on 7 February 1947 (*W T Larkins*)

LIBERATOR LINER

Knowing that the post-war airline market would be greatly expanded, Consolidated attempted to convert the Liberator design into an airliner. This would not be a conversion of a bomber into a passenger hauler, but rather an attempt to create a modern and comfortable passenger liner. Given the company designation of Model 39, it was decided to use the wings, engines, landing gear and tail section of the PB4Y-2. A new 90-ft long fuselage with a 10.6-ft diameter would be built that could house 48 day passengers or 24 Pullman-style sleepers. A dedicated cargo variant was also proposed that could lift 18,500 lbs of supplies (a large cargo door was built into the left rear fuselage).

This was a private venture project by the company, and in early 1944 the completed fuselage was shipped to San Diego, where it was mated with the requisite Privateer bits and pieces. At this point no interest had been shown by the airlines or the military, but on 20 March 1944 the Navy issued a letter of intent to procure 253 Model 39s with the military designation R2Y-1. However, a solid order did not materialise, despite the prototype Model 39 being completed in Navy markings with the designation XR2Y-1 and Bureau Number 09803. The Navy had assigned the Bureau Number to Consolidated so that the company could in turn start test flying the aeroplane on 15 April 1944, with Phil Prophett in command.

Finished as the US Navy's XR2Y-1, the Model 39 was photographed on a test flight from San Diego in mid 1944. The graceful cylindrical fuselage is apparent in this high-angle view, and it blends in nicely with the Davis wing. Later in its life the XR2Y-1 received fancy trim and the name *LIBERATOR-LINER* on the rear fuselage

After flight testing had started, the Navy inspected the aircraft and found it deficient in a number of areas. The intrusion of the wing spars through the circular fuselage was not found acceptable, nor was its estimated take-off performance with a full load. Also, a full load could not be carried because of the original bomber landing gear, so a new gear system would have to be devised. Also, the Navy reasoned that the Model 39 did not have any growth potential.

However, work had started on the first R2Y-1 in anticipation of a Navy contract, and this incomplete airframe was purchased by Consolidated and finished with R-1830-65 engines. It was first flown on 29 September 1944, with civil registration NX3939. In the meantime, the prototype received the civil registration NX30039, and the name *LIBERATOR-LINER* was applied to its fuselage.

Trying to sell the Liberator Liner to American Airlines, Consolidated entered into a three-month agreement starting in July 1945 that saw NX30039, named *City of Salinas* and finished in American markings, operating on a single flight between Chicago and Los Angeles with a load of gas ovens. Subsequent flights were made from Salinas and El Centro, California, to New York and Boston with significant quantities of fresh fruit and vegetables.

Try as they might, however, Consolidated could not find a buyer for the aircraft (which had been redesignated the Convair Model 104), and both were duly scrapped during September 1945.

ICE CUBES FOR JAPAN!

Listen, Tojo—when you hear that *kar-rump* some night and the factory walls start sliding into the sea—look out, it's one of those new "ice cubes" from Nash-Kelvinator!

We are building *plenty* of them just for you—huge Kelvinators that fly and ice cubes that hurt.

Monster metal-bellied flying boats—growing on Nash-Kelvinator assembly lines—to whisk the Navy's men and material to any spot you raise your head! Giant Vought-Sikorsky cargo carriers built *complete*—and not in ones or twos, but in fleet upon fleet!

Want to hear some more?

Then listen—that angry hum coming out of the East—

They are the propellers built by Nash-Kelvinator, built by the many thousands!

And that mighty roar you'll soon be hearing is the voice of the most powerful engine ever placed in a pursuit ship. It will take the Navy's new *Corsair* higher, faster than any "Zero" in your stable.

They're coming, Tojo—coming from men who, in building last year's refrigerators and automobiles, thought only of a nation's health and happiness.

But now, it's hate and vengeance and the remembrance of a thousand Axis wrongs that are guiding their hands . . . beating every production record in Nash-Kelvinator history by two and three.

Look out, Tojo, *the nights are growing longer.*   •   •   •

NASH-KELVINATOR CORPORATION

NASH ⬛ KELVINATOR

PRATT & WHITNEY
HIGH-ALTITUDE
ENGINES

VOUGHT-SIKORSKY
FLYING BOATS

HAMILTON
STANDARD
PROPELLERS

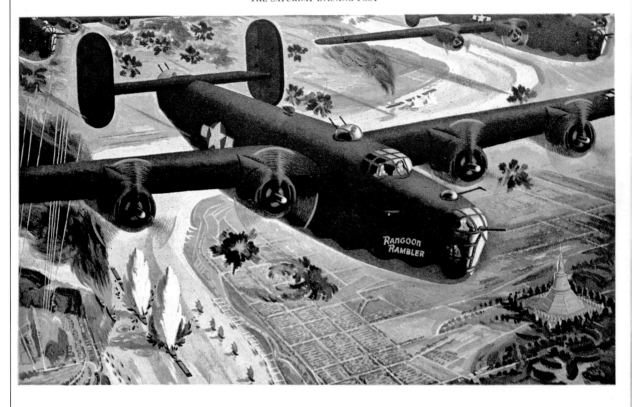

The "Rambler" Roars into Rangoon

This morning you're flying with the crew of the famous "Rangoon Rambler" . . .

Crouched in the glassed-in nose beside you, Lt. Guy Spotts, the navigator, studies a map spread across his knees, checks off landmarks as they slide past underneath. Suddenly he peers ahead . . . speaks into his throat-microphone: "Pilot from navigator. There she is, Rote. We can see the target now. Alter course to three-three-zero."

"Roger!" Capt. Raymond Rote, the pilot, eases the big B-24 around and straightens out on his new course.

Then *you* see it . . . a splash of flame against the green horizon . . . the great, gold-domed Shwe Dagôn Pagoda that towers over Rangoon. You're getting close . . . and the crew gets set. Lt. Robert Currie, the bombardier, fiddles with the knobs on his bombsight. Capt. Gordon Wilson, co-pilot, gives the instruments a last-minute check.

Now you're over the target . . . a flock of pot-bellied Jap cargo ships squatting there in the river's bend. The "Rambler" lurches and bucks as she ducks through bursts of ack-ack and goes into her bombing run.

Your heart pounds hard. Then Currie comes in on the intercom . . . cool as if he were ordering cokes at the Assam Officers' Club: "Pilot from bombardier. Bombs away! Let's get out of here, pal!"

Looking back and below, you watch the formation's bombs bullseye the target. A freighter goes up in a blast of fire and black smoke. The ship beside it explodes. Flames break out from a third. And a fourth. Currie and the other bombardiers were "on the beam" today.

Rote banks the Lib around steep, and you high-tail for home. You're congratulating yourself when . . . "Fighters at four o'clock—high!" somebody yells. You look up and see a formation of Japs sweeping out of the sun.

Now it's the gunners' turn. And between squirts of their big, twin-50's they keep up a running pep-talk:

"There goes his wing down! He's coming in! This one's *my* meat, Salley!"

"Hey, skipper—kick her over a little. I want a good shot at this guy."

And two Japs spiral down in flames, and the rest decide to quit. That's all for today. You look around at the crew, relaxing now, shooting the breeze, adding up the score. You think of the ribbons each man has won for flights like this.

And it makes your chest puff out with pride to be flying with guys like these . . . to be wearing the wings of the A.A.F.—the "greatest team in the world!"

U. S. ARMY RECRUITING SERVICE

THE "RANGOON RAMBLERS": Standing: Sgt. Ferdinand Knechtel, gunner; Capt. Raymond Rote; Capt. Gordon Wilson; Lt. Guy Spotts; Lt. Robert Currie; Sgt. Joseph Willis, gunner. Seated: Sgt. John Craigie, Sgt. Carl Paak, Sgt. Adolph Scolavino, Sgt. Edward Salley, gunners.

MEN OF 17

. . . if *you* want to fly on a team like the "Rangoon Ramblers" . . . as Navigator, Bombardier, Pilot or Gunner . . . go to your nearest Aviation Cadet Examining Board . . . see if you can qualify for the Air Corps Enlisted Reserve. If you qualify, you will receive this insignia . . . but will not be called for training until you are 18 or over.

When called, your special apti-tudes will be studied further to determine the type of training you will receive. For the A.A.F. carefully selects for each position on a combat crew the man best qualified for the job . . . and then adds the thorough training which makes this all-star team the world's finest.

For pre-aviation training, see your local Civil Air Patrol officers. Also see your High School Principal or Adviser about recommended courses in the Air Service Division of the High School Victory Corps.

(Essential workers in War Industry or Agriculture—do not apply.)

 KEEP 'EM FLYING! For information on Naval Aviation Cadet Training, apply at nearest Office of Naval Officer Procurement. This advertisement has the approval of the Joint Army Navy Personnel Board.

FLY AND FIGHT WITH THE **AAF** ARMY AIR FORCES GREATEST TEAM IN THE WORLD

THROUGH TRUSCON STEEL HANGAR DOORS—

a mighty flock of man-made eagles!

When these deadly American bombers come off the assembly line, chances are they roll out into service through Truscon Steel Hangar Doors.

For a large percentage of American aircraft manufacturing and assembly plants are equipped with swift, maneuverable Truscon door units. These steel doors are built in wide sections, that can be combined to permit obstruction-free traffic across any required width or height.

Today, along with Truscon roofdeck, sidewalls and other airplane factory and hangar construction units, Truscon Steel Hangar Doors are helping to speed essential war production. Tomorrow, they will be an important part of America's great civil and commercial expansion into the skyways of the world. Truscon Steel Company, Youngstown, Ohio.

TRUSCON STEEL COMPANY
SUBSIDIARY OF REPUBLIC STEEL CORPORATION

HE THUMBED HIS B-24 NOSE
at a torrent of hot Nazi steel

A true story of sixty thrill-packed seconds in the life of an American flyer whose armor weathered a deadly hail of machine gun fire to save his life.

He was parked in the nose turret of a B-24 Liberator—part of a formation of Allied bombers bent on destruction of a critical Nazi war area. High above the clouds, his plane droned nearer and nearer its target.

Suddenly, he caught a fleeting glimpse of a cloud-hopping Nazi fighter plane. Trigger fingers became tense and in a flash the scrap was on.

Streaking out of a cloud at lightning speed, the Heinie bored in with his guns spitting fire and steel. The aim was deadly. CRASH went the plastic panes of the turret and a fusillade of steel poured in. But the Nazi slugs were plunking into a tough wall of armor—*and they didn't get through!*

BUY MORE THAN BEFORE
in the 5th War Loan Drive

All the while the B-24's nose guns were blazing a stream of fire—*and hitting their mark.* Doggedly the Nazi fighter dove in again. Smack on the nose came another hail of hot steel— *and again the guard of armor stopped it cold.*

Finally, the steady fire from the Yankee guns ripped through a vital spot—the Nazi fighter pilot went crashing to his death. And thanks to the B-24's fighting armor, the kid in the nose turret came through *without a scratch.*

* * *

This incident gives Van Dorn workers a glowing sense of pride. For they are among the builders of armor for the nose turrets of the B-24. They are producing armor plate that guards the flyers of almost all types of American fighter and bomber planes. And their skill in applying our 65 years of metal fabricating experience to the building of stronger armor protection is reflected in the high percentage of our flyers *who are returning safely.*

A tale like this should be an inspiration to every man and woman in war work to do a better job in backing the men at the fighting fronts. For tomorrow, their lives may depend upon how fast and how well we do our jobs today.

THE VAN DORN
IRON WORKS COMPANY · CLEVELAND 4, O.

SPECIALISTS IN METAL FABRICATION
AND HEAT TREATMENT SINCE 1878

Night Patrol

"WE were flying routine night patrol," said the bomber pilot, in relating the incident which won for him a letter of commendation from the Commanding General. "Flying at 1000 feet, we saw the sub surface. Descending to 300 feet and flying at 300 miles per hour, we switched on our landing lights; and as we passed over the sub, bracketed it with four depth charges."

In accordance with Army regulations, names are omitted in this story from COMMAND POST, McClellan Field, Calif.

This is the G-E Airplane landing lamp—*generally used for safer landings, but employed by this pilot to help blast a sub. Built in the same way as your G-E Sealed Beam headlamps, it is only one of over 200 lamps used on the average big bomber.*

To make lamps STAY BRIGHTER LONGER
THE CREED OF G-E RESEARCH

When the last patrol has flown and the lights come on again, General Electric Research will be seeking new ways to bring you brighter, happier living. Health-giving ultra-violet . . . fluorescent "daylight" for kitchen or bedroom . . . and other new applications of light. Right now so many G-E lamps are serving our fighting forces that it is important to make the most of the lamp bulbs you have. Keep your G-E Mazda lamps clean, keep them close when you read or work, and turn them off when not in use. Conserve for Victory!

G·E MAZDA LAMPS
GENERAL ⓖⓔ ELECTRIC

Hear the General Electric radio programs "The G-E All-Girl Orchestra", Sunday 10 p. m. EWT, NBC; "The World Today" news, every weekday 6:45 p. m. EWT, CBS.

BUY BONDS FOR VICTORY

Consolidated Liberator

HOW DO YOU LIKE 'EM, MR. HITLER?

Posters of this illustration, 25" x 38", are offered in quantity, with all space below illustration left blank for your own message and signature. Write Aluminum Company of America, 1999 Gulf Building, Pittsburgh, Pennsylvania.

The thousands of planes winging their way this month to all corners of the earth are a very special message from the men and women of Alcoa Aluminum, delivered via the plane-makers and the best fliers in the world. You never figured, did you, *Mister* Hitler and *Mister* Yamamoto, that just this one outfit, sixty thousand Americans with an awful lot of know-how, would be able to push out so much metal to make so many planes so soon? And the thousands are on their way to becoming ten thousands. Perhaps you didn't take it very seriously when our outfit started building big new plants long before we were actually in this war. More than once they had us turning out the aluminum before the roofs were on. All we can say, Mr. H & Mr. Y, is that you made one awful mistake about this outfit. But you're finding out!

The men and women of ALCOA ALUMINUM

CHAPTER 3 THE KING'S LIBERATORS

An impressive line-up of Liberator IIs at Consolidated's San Diego, California, factory in late 1941. A censor had carefully gone through the line up and removed all the serials from the negative! However, the lead aircraft is AL590. The open hatches atop the fuselage are where life rafts would be fitted. The Liberators were camouflaged in standard Bomber Command colours of Dark Earth, Dark Green and Black

WITH HITLER'S rapid expansion, surviving European countries were especially interested in obtaining large quantities of combat aircraft. France, which had developed a large, but not particularly effective, air force had a purchasing commission in the United States examining a variety of military aeroplanes being made by various countries. After examining the XB-24 and the Consolidated plant, the French Purchasing Commission contracted for 175 aircraft in April 1940. The type was designated within Consolidated's 'Land Bomber' series as the LB-30MF (Mission *Francais*).

It is rather difficult to understand what France was thinking. Although the bombers could be completed in a relatively quickly, there was insufficient time available to either train crews to fly them or form squadrons to operate them in the frontline. When

the Nazis moved against France, they moved quickly, and the hope of a heavy bomber to use against the invaders was relegated into the realms of fantasy.

Also short of modern heavy bombers, Britain hastily took over 135 of these aircraft, with the designation LB-30 Liberator, following the fall of France in June 1940. However, the RAF realised that the aircraft had a distinct problem that would prevent them from entering combat in the hostile skies of Europe – they lacked self-sealing fuel tanks. This effectively meant that just one solitary bullet through a fuel tank could turn the bomber into a flaming torch. The LB-30's defensive equipment was also less than impressive, so six 0.50-cal Brownings were added in strategic positions. Following this hasty modification, six LB-30As became to first Liberators to actually enter service.

Flown across the Atlantic, the aircraft were then stripped of their armament and a rough passenger interior fitted, along with extra oxygen, airframe de-icing and extra heaters, to enable the LB-30s to operate on a regular shuttle service between the UK and North America. The aircraft were assigned to Ferry Command in March 1941 and carried serials AM258 through to AM263. Transatlantic missions began on 4 May 1941 between Blackpool and Montreal, and these aircraft went on to perform heroic service, heading back and forth across the hostile Atlantic carrying vital cargo, VIPs and ferry crews.

Desperate to obtain a combat variant of the Liberator, the British government hastily struck a deal to obtain 20 B-24s built for the Army which had self-sealing tanks and other equipment considered much more suitable for combat against the Germans. The Army would receive 20 LB-30s in return, which could be used for training and transport duties.

Flight testing revealed that with proper power management these aircraft could remain airborne for 16 hours, which made the Liberator an ideal weapon to use against the U-boat threat. Initially designated LB-30B 'B-24 Conversion', the aircraft became the Liberator Mk I in operational service.

Never particularly pleased with the standard American armament, the RAF decided to optimise the Liberators for its war against the U-boat menace. Ten Mk Is were sent to Scottish Aviation, Prestwick, for modifications to fight an enemy that was draining Britain's life blood, and the company quickly designed a tray that was to be installed under the forward fuselage. This would hold four 20 mm Hispano cannon firing directly forward. Consideration was also given to a Martin-Baker design to fit a solid nose on the aircraft which would be fitted with 12 0.303-in machines guns. The Hispano installation won out, but Martin-Baker built at least one B-25 Mitchell nose fitted with the dozen machine guns. This gave the aircraft a tremendous punch against the thin-skinned submarines.

To help in the search for an elusive enemy, ASV radar was installed, and this early unit required numerous antennas to be grafted onto the fuselage and wings.

The modified Liberators went into service at Nutts Corner, Northern Ireland, with No 120 Sqn in June 1941, and the aircraft began setting out on very long range patrols against the U-boats in the north Atlantic three months later. Right from the start, the Liberator's excellent range, cannon armament and bomb-bay load of depth charges or bombs began to do damage to Hitler's submarines. At this time, Luftwaffe Focke-Wulf Fw 200 Kondors were also attacking convoys, and the crews of No 120 Sqn hoped that they would engage one of the long-range patrol bombers. Just such an encounter occurred in October when Liberator AM924 attacked an Fw 200. Hits were seen on the enemy aircraft, which quickly departed the area.

Given their small numbers, these modified Liberators were very effective, and following their introduction into service, the success rate of the U-boats began to decline. Of the remaining batch of 20 'B-24A Conversions', a few more were modified for Coastal Command with updated radar, while the remainder were used as transports or trainers.

RAF Liberators versus the U-boat

U-boat	Date	Aircraft	Serial	Unit	Location
U-597	12/10/42	Mk I	AM929	120	Off Iceland
U-61	15/10/42	Mk I	AM929	120	Off Iceland
U-216	20/10/42	Mk III	FL910	224	Off Iceland
U-599	24/10/42	MkIII	FL910	224	Off Azores
U-132	5/11/42	Mk I	AM929	120	?
U-529	15/1/43	Mk ?	?	120	Cape Farewell
U-623	21/1/43	Mk ?	?	120	?
U-189	23/1/43	Mk ?	?	120	Off Iceland
U-266	14/2/43	Mk ?	?	86	?
U-109	23/2/43	Mk ?	?	86	Off Ireland
U-632	6/4/43	Mk IIIA	?	86	?
U-258	20/4/43	Mk I	AM919	120	?
U-304	28/4/43	Mk I	AM919	120	?
U-465	4/5/43	Mk IIIA	?	86	?
U-266	14/5/43	Mk IIIA	?	86	?
U-954	19/5/43	Mk ?	?	120	?
U-194	24/6/43	Mk I	AM929	120	Off Iceland
U-628	3/7/43	Mk I	?	224	?
U-535	5/7/43	Mk V	?	53	Bay of Biscay
U-514	8/7/43	Mk V	?	224	Bay of Biscay
U-404	28/7/43	Mk ?	?	224	Bay of Biscay
U-468	11/8/43	Mk V	?	200	Near Bathurst
U-403	17/8/43	Mk V	BZ832	200	Near Dakar
U-341	19/9/43	GR V	BZ732	10 RCAF	North Atlantic
U-338	20/9/43	Mk III	FL910	120	Near Iceland
U-279	4/10/43	Mk ?	?	120	Near Iceland
U-419	8/10/43	Mk III	?	86	Near Iceland

U-boat	Date	Aircraft	Serial	Unit	Location
U-470	16/10/43	Mk III	FK223	120	Near Iceland
U-844	16/10/43	Mk V	?	59	Near Iceland
U-964	16/10/43	Mk V	?	86	Near Iceland
U-540	17/10/43	Mk I	AM929	120	Cape Farewell
U-274	23/10/43	Mk I	?	224	?
U-420	26/10/43	GR V	BZ732	10 RCAF	North Atlantic
U-66	10/11/43	Mk ?	?	311 'Czech'	?.
U-280	16/11/43	Mk ?	?	86	?
U-391	13/12/43	Mk V	?	53	?
U-601	25/2/44	Mk ?	?	120	?
U-990	25/5/44	Mk V	?	59	?
U-292	27/5/44	Mk V	?	59	?
U-?	7/6/44	Mk V	BZ944	53	Off England
U-629	8/6/44	GR V	?	224	?
U-373	8/6/44	GR V	?	224	?
U-740	9/6/44	Mk ?	?	120	?
U-821	10/6/44	Mk VI	EV943	206	?
U-971	24/6/44	Mk VI	?	311 'Czech'	?
U-317	26/6/44	Mk V	?	86	?
U-988	29/6/44	Mk ?	?	224	?
U-478	30/6/44	Mk ?	?	86	?
U-243	8/7/44	Mk ?	?	10 RCAF	Bay of Biscay
U-319	15/7/44	Mk VI	?	86	?
U-361	17/7/44	Mk ?	?	86	?
U-?	30/7/44	Mk ?	?	53	?
U-618	14/8/44	Mk ?	?	53	?
U-608	19/8/44	Mk ?	?	53	?
U-865	14/9/44	Mk VI	BZ984	206	?
U-867	19/9/44	Mk ?	?	224	?
U-855	24/9/44	Mk ?	?	224	?
U-1060	29/10/44	Mk ?	?	311 'Czech'	?
U-905	20/3/45	Mk VI	?	86	?
U-296	22/3/45	Mk VIII	?	120	?
U-1106	29/3/45	Mk VIII	?	224	?
U-1276	3/4/45	Mk VIII	?	224	?
U-396	23/4/45	Mk VI	?	86	?
U-1017	29/4/45	Mk VIII	?	120	?
U-3523	5/5/45	Mk ?	?	224	?
U-534	5/5/45	Mk VIII	KK250	206	?
U-2365	5/5/45	Mk ?	?	311	?
U-2521	5/5/45	Mk ?	?	547	?
U-3503	5/5/45	Mk ?	?	86	?
U-2534	6/5/45	Mk ?	?	86	?
U-1008	6/5/45	Mk ?	?	86	?

The next variant obtained was purchased exclusively for Bomber Command, and it was designated Liberator Mk II. This was basically a British version of the B-24C, which had the 'stretched' nose section and was fitted with civilian R-1830-S3C4-G (military variant R-1830-61) engines uniquely driving Curtiss Electric propellers. These aeroplanes were delivered directly from San Diego to Britain, although 75 airframes (of which about two dozen would eventually be returned to the RAF) from the order were hastily taken over by the USAAF. On 17 January 1942 the 7th Bombardment Group, flying ex-RAF Liberator Mk IIs, became the first US B-24 unit to go into action when they attacked a Japanese airfield in Java. In British service, the Mk II bristled with 14 0.303-in guns, including Boulton Paul upper and tail powered turrets, and the aircraft went into action with No 108 Sqn in the Middle East on 10 January 1942.

As with the aircraft in USAAF service, as soon as newer variants were available, the earlier RAF Liberators would be shuffled off to second-line duties. The Mk III was essentially a B-24D with British equipment and armament, and it was also the first RAF Liberator with turbosupercharged engines, which gave the aircraft its characteristic oval-shaped nacelles. The Mk III usually – but not always – had the Martin tail turret replaced with a Boulton Paul unit fitted with four 0.303-in machine guns, while the belly turret was often eliminated and faired over. Mk IIIs were also assigned to Coastal Command, where additional fuel tanks were installed to increase range and some equipment not necessary for the ASW mission removed to save weight.

Up to this point, Liberators had been supplied to the British via direct purchase, but starting with the Mk IIIA the aircraft would come from Lend-Lease contracts. Even though

Photographed on the ramp at East Boston Airport, Massachusetts, Mk II AL507 boasts an SCR-517 centimetric radar scanner in a nose radome. This modification led to these modified Mk IIs being nicknamed 'Dumbo' by the crews that flew and maintained them. The aircraft is also fitted with the mid-fuselage Boulton Paul turret that housed four 0.303-in machine guns. AL507 served with a variety of frontline and training units prior to being passed on to BOAC on 1 August 1944. The airline stripped the bomber of its ASW gear and placed it in service as G-AHYC

the Mk IV was essentially similar to the Mk III, it was given a separate designation because it was built at the new Ford factory. North American-built B-24Gs became GR Vs, while B-24H/Js were designated GR VIs with Coastal Command. Once again optimised for range, some of these aircraft were modified with Leigh Lights (mounted in a pod, this unit weight 870 lb and generated a narrow beam with 19 million candlepower for about a mile) to illuminate targets at night, while others were fitted with rocket rails that protruded from stub wings on the sides of the forward fuselage.

The C Mk VII was the RAF variant of the purpose-built C-87 transport, and these aircraft were obtained in the latter stages of the war. The GR Mk VIII was very similar to the Mk VI, but with detail modifications, and it was the last Liberator variant to be obtained by Coastal Command.

The Liberator's contribution to Coastal Command's campaign against the U-boat was extremely important to the outcome of the war, for the aircraft and its crews effectively blunted the threat posed by the once mighty German submarine force.

Photographed at Aldergrove, in Northern Ireland, this impressive line-up of Coastal Command Liberators is led by GR Mk III FK228 of No 120 Sqn, which is fitted with large antennas on the sides of the fuselage and under the wing for ASW radar. During the war, No 120 Sqn flew six different variants of Liberators, and by the end of the war the unit had 16 confirmed U-boat victories to its credit, making it the highest-scoring squadron in Coastal Command

A beautiful aerial view of Liberator Mk III FL927/G (the G indicated that the aircraft needed to be under constant armed guard while on the ground in order to protect the new equipment then being tested) displaying its forward fuselage stub wings, which would hold rockets for attacking enemy targets. Coastal Command found the hand-held machine guns in the nose inadequate for pressing home attacks on U-boats and shipping, hence the rockets

Liberator GR Mk VI BZ963 carries the standard USAAF data block on the nose – a requirement for Lend-Lease aircraft. The addition of the nose turret significantly increased the potency of the Liberator when attacking shipping or surfaced U-boats. Delivered to the RAF in late 1943, BZ963 saw frontline service with No 59 Sqn from Ballykelly, in Northern Ireland

Liberator GR Mk VI EV834 of No 354 Sqn is seen in its environment – down low over the Indian Ocean. Note its South East Asia Command markings

The RAF deployed its Liberator VIs as heavy bombers in the Far East and Middle East, where they were very successful in mine dropping and strategic bombing. As the war neared its end the RAF received some Liberator C Mk IXs which were single-tail RY-3s. With the end of the war, Liberators took on the task of flying British PoWs home from all corners of the world.

As with the USAAF, RAF Liberators were quickly phased out of service (although some Coastal Command aircraft remained operational until 1947), and under the terms of Lend-Lease, the aircraft had to either be returned, purchased or scrapped. Britain had received 1694 Liberators of various marks, many of which were gathered in India post-war and scrapped.

However, the British did not really do a thorough job, as engineers from Hindustan Aircraft Ltd went through the scrap yards and managed to resurrect 16 Liberators, which were brought back to flying status and modified for the maritime patrol role. Amazingly, these aircraft flew successfully with the Indian Air Force's No 6 Sqn until finally retired in 1967.

BOMBER COMMAND LIBERATOR SQUADRONS

MTO – Nos 37, 40, 70, 104, 178 Sqns, No 1586 'Polish' Special Duties Flight and No 334 Special Duty Wing.

INDIA – No 159 Sqn

SOUTH EAST ASIA – Nos 99, 159, 215, 355 and 356 Sqns

ETO – Nos 108, 148, 160, 214, 223, 358 and 614 Sqns

COASTAL COMMAND LIBERATOR SQUADRONS

WEST AFRICA – No 200 Sqn

BERMUDA – No 231 Sqn (post-war only)

INDIA – Nos 160, 200, 203, 232, 321 and 354 Sqns

SOUTH EAST ASIA – No 52 Sqn

ETO – Nos 53, 59, 86, 120, 206, 220, 224, 228 (post-war only), 246, 422 (post-war only), 423 (post-war only), 511 and 547 Sqns

Liberator Mk VIII KH228 displays its AN/APS-15 search radar, which replaced the bomber's belly turret. Issued to No 614 Sqn at Amendola, in Italy, in late 1944, this aircraft survived the war in Europe only to be damaged beyond repair at Cairo West on 22 June 1945. The bomber had just taken off when it sank back and hit the runway, causing the nosewheel to collapse

CHAPTER 4

FRONTLINE

The Air Corps received its nine B-24As between June and July 1941, and the aircraft were delivered in standard RAF camouflage, but most of the A-models were also marked with large 'neutrality' flags on the forward fuselage and atop the centre section of the fuselage, making for a most distinctive colour scheme. B-24A USAAC s/n 40-2374 was one of two Liberators utilised by Ferrying Command to haul W Averell Harriman and his party to Moscow during September 1941. Harriman was the special envoy to the USSR and UK on assignment for President Franklin Roosevelt. This aircraft was piloted during the long range shuttle flights by Louis Reicher, a well-known pre-war pilot. The Liberator is seen here shortly after landing at Sembawang Airport, in Singapore, on 30 October 1941 on its return trip to the United States after the epic mission to discuss Lend-Lease with the Soviets. Note the air stair door that had been built into the fuselage forward of the pre-war national insignia. These aircraft did not carry armament

ABOVE With the advent of the B-24D, the Liberator finally became an operational bomber. Powered by R-1830-43s, the first example was rolled out of the San Diego factory on 22 January 1942. This unidentified B-24 was photographed at Gander Airfield, Newfoundland, in May 1943 during its ferry flight to the MTO, where it would serve as an attrition replacement for the Liberator force then involved in attacks on Axis oilfields in Rumania. The aircraft was camouflaged in Sand (officially known as Sand shade 49 and unofficially as 'Desert Pink' or 'Titty Pink') and Neutral Gray for desert operations. Note the short-lived Red surround to the national insignia, which was introduced on 29 June 1943

One of the most dramatic photographs to come out of America's early days at war was this shot of massed Liberators hitting the Rumanian refineries at Ploesti on 1 August 1943 as part of Operation *Tidal Wave*. Of the 197 Liberators that launched on this mission from bases in North Africa, 14 aborted or crashed before they reached Ploesti, and 165 succeeded in bombing enemy targets. Flak destroyed a further 34 B-24s while Axis fighters downed 13, for a total loss of 532 American aircrew. The losses were heavy but the enemy's oil refineries had received significant damage

ABOVE Five Liberator groups took part in Operation *Tidal Wave*, namely the 93rd BG 'Ted's Traveling Circus', 44th BG 'Eight Balls', 389th BG 'Sky Scorpions', 98th BG 'Pyramiders' and 376th BG 'Liberandos'. Carrying many personal markings and battle awards, *The Squaw* heads home for a War Bond tour. B-24D USAAF s/n 41-1176, like the other Liberators of the 98th BG, was finished in the Sand and Neutral Gray camouflage scheme prevalent in the MTO in 1942-43. On its arrival in the US, the bomber's scoreboard revealed that it had dropped 360,000 lbs of bombs on Axis targets in Africa, Sicily, Italy, Greece, Crete and Rumania during the course of 71 combat missions (550 hours). Its gunners had also claimed six enemy fighters destroyed

ABOVE The air war in the Aleutians was deadly – both the enemy and the weather took a heavy toll of the American aircraft stationed in one of the remotest parts of the world. The islands of Kiska and Attu were the only American territory captured by the Japanese during World War 2. Starting in August 1942, Eleventh Air Force Liberators operating from Alaska began strikes against Kiska, and when airfields were built on Amchitka and Adak, raids could be launched against enemy forces on Attu as well. This veteran 404th BS/28th BG B-24D USAAF s/n 41-23848 was photographed parked on PSP (Pierced Steel Planking) at Shemya Army Air Force Base in April 1944. Upon their arrival in Alaska, the 404th's Liberators were dubbed 'Pink Elephants' because many of them were painted in Sand and Neutral Gray camouflage. This particular aircraft crashed in the sea off Agattu Island on 12 June 1944 (*Norm Taylor*)

ABOVE 404th BS 'Pink Elephants' B-24D USAAF s/n 43-73035 burns at Shemya on 19 August 1944 following a crash landing. During the course of the war, the 28th BG flew nearly 2600 missions and lost 33 aircraft in action. A further 22 Liberators were recorded as written off in non-combat related accidents. In return, B-24 gunners from the group claimed 29 Japanese aircraft shot down

'This is how you do it.' A Luftwaffe instructor shows his students how to attack B-24Ds head-on with their Fw 190s. The hand-held weapons in the nose of the B-24D were a weak point on the aircraft. Note how the fields of fire from the other gun positions have been defined

B-24D USAAF s/n 41-28667 *Jayhawker* watches over a group of Bell P-39 Airacobras fitted with long range tanks. Assigned to the 752nd BS/458th BG, it is possible that the Liberator was serving as a navigation ship for the delivery of the P-39s to the MTO

ABOVE B-24D-1-CO USAAF s/n 41-23728, assigned to the Tenth Air Force, was photographed over India in June 1943 while on a test flight. The Liberator had been left behind by Gen Lewis Brereton's forces when they abandoned their airfield due to advancing Japanese troops. However, another USAAF unit repaired the B-24 and got it back into the air (*L Somnen*)

ABOVE Nearly factory-fresh B-24J USAAF s/n 44-40052 features full markings for the 565th BS/389th BG, including the group's distinctive bright green vertical tails. After its famous strike on Ploesti, the 389th returned to Britain before temporarily deploying to the MTO once again. After returning to Britain for a second time, the unit operated against strategic targets until VE-Day. The highlights of the 389th's time in the ETO included participation in Operation *Big Week* (20-25 February 1944), the Normandy Invasion, the Saint-Lo Breakout, the Battle of the Bulge and supply missions for Allied troops crossing the Rhine. The unit flew its last combat sorties on 25 April 1945 and returned home between May and June of that year. The 389th was inactivated at Charleston, South Carolina, on 13 September 1945 (*Fred Freeman*)

Incredibly weathered B-24D-120-CO USAAF s/n 42-41157 displays its rather unattractive Oklahoma City Modification Center nose turret installation. The aircraft was assigned to the Eleventh Air Force's 404th BS, and was photographed over Shemya on 1 November 1945 (*Norm Taylor*)

An irate (and anonymous) squadron commander in the ETO ordered this lettering added to the inside tail fins of his unit's Liberators after waist gunners had made a few 'mistakes' in the heat of battle!

ABOVE The wildly painted *Spotted Ape* of the 458th BG was employed as an assembly ship for the group, these combat-weary veterans being used to help form up formations prior to the B-24s heading for Occupied Europe. Paint schemes such as this one made the aircraft an easy target for Liberator crews as they assembled in their box formations. The *Spotted Ape* was photographed at the group's Horsham St Faith base, in Norfolk, on 9 March 1945

LEFT A 458th BG Liberator explodes in flames after being hit by flak during a raid on railway marshalling yards in Munich, Germany

BELOW Painted overall black, B-24J USAAF s/n 42-51311 *"TAR BABY"* certainly lived up to its name. Assigned to Lt Paul Pond's crew, the Liberator belonged to the 36th BS, which was a unique unit whose duties included the jamming of enemy radar, screening of USAAF VHF channels while bombers were assembling, carrying out spoof raids, jamming enemy tank communications and performing special electronic search missions

ABOVE B-24D USAAF s/n 42-72956 *Betsy* was operated by the 321st BS/90th BG, and boasts the group's famed 'Jolly Rogers' insignia on its vertical fin. The 90th's nickname came from the leadership style of Col Roger Ramey who took command of the unit on 14 September 1942. The group arrived at Iron Range, Australia, in November 1942, and went into combat attacking Japanese troop concentrations, airfields, ground installations and shipping in the New Guinea area

ABOVE Although destroyed in this crash-landing, the B-24H's crew all escaped unscathed. Assigned to the 389th BG, the battle damaged Liberator had struggled back to its base at Hethel, in Norfolk, where quick-acting rescue crews prevented a fire from breaking out

ABOVE Despite having suffered minor flak damage to the rear fuselage, this Liberator from the 705th BS/446th BG pressed on to its target in the Austrian mountains and dropped its load of three 1000-lb bombs. Note that the upper turret gunner is poised ready for action

ABOVE *Ruthless Ruthie* was Consolidated-built B-24J-155-CO USAAF s/n 44-40317. Assigned to the 854th BS/491st BG, the aircraft had its right main tyre damaged by flak during a mission to Germany in September 1944, and upon landing back at North Pickenham the tyre blew out and the bomber viciously ground looped. The crew hastily evacuated the aircraft, as evidenced by the numerous hatches scattered around the B-24. Note that this natural metal bomber has had its national insignia 'toned down' with a grey wash by an official decree

ABOVE B-24J USAAF s/n 44-40275 *"SHACK TIME"* leads a group of 458th BG Liberators on a mission to Germany. This aircraft was equipped with AZON (AZimuth ONly) AN/ARW-9 bombing equipment, which permitted the bombardier to steer bombs laterally. *"SHACK TIME"* was eventually written off in a flying accident on 14 November 1944

LEFT It was not uncommon for waist gunners to deploy their parachutes to slow a Liberator down after landing should the bomber's hydraulic system have been knocked out by enemy fire. Douglas-built B-24H USAAF s/n 42-51141 *Pegasus, the Flying Red Horse* experienced just such a landing at its Attlebridge, Norfolk, base in late 1944. Assigned to the 784th BS/466th BG, this aircraft survived a year-long tour in the ETO and returned to the USA after completing 42 missions

ABOVE At least 80 Liberators were modified for 'Carpetbagger' operations – the dropping of agents over occupied territory. The ball turret was removed and some of the surrounding metal cut away to create a 'Joe Hole', and a wind shield was installed so that agents could safely jump from the aircraft. A hardpoint was installed in the fuselage for the parachute static lines and red dome lights were installed inside the fuselage so not to damage the agents' night vision. The nose compartment was extensively modified, with the turret removed to provide a better working environment for the bombardier and navigator. Flame dampners were also added to the engine exhausts and the aircraft were painted overall black. Agents were known as 'Joes', 'Janes' or 'Josephines', depending on their gender. Modified Liberators (initially D-models) were employed on these clandestine missions from January 1944 until war's end. In this photo, agents don their parachutes and other equipment while 'Carpetbagger' B-24s await their human cargo

LEFT Finished in gloss anti-searchlight black, 'Carpetbagger' B-24H s/n 42-51211 of the 492nd BG takes off at the start of a mission from Harrington, in Northamptonshire, under the command of Lt Paul Carr. The aircraft's modified nose section is clearly evident

ABOVE With its bombs spilling from its ruptured bomb-bay, a 465th BG Liberator disintegrates after receiving a direct flak hit in the fuel tanks during its approach to Blechhammer, in Germany, in late 1944

BELOW Returning with honour. Engines throttled back, the pilot slightly raises the nose as he flares his B-24J of the 564th BS/ 389th BG just a moment before touchdown at Bradley Field, Connecticut, in May 1945. The aircraft had just completed a transatlantic crossing – a lot of trouble for a war-weary bomber that would subsequently be placed in a storage yard and duly sold off for scrap
(Lt Col Mike Moffitt)

ABOVE The first Liberators delivered to the US Navy were simply B-24Ds still in full USAAF markings and Olive Drab and Neutral Gray camouflage schemes. Indeed, the only way they could be identified as PB4Y-1s was by the underlined designation and Bureau Number (31337) placed above the USAAF serial (41-23827) on the vertical tail surfaces. This particular aircraft was the second Liberator delivered to the Navy by Consolidated

ABOVE As with the USAAF, the Navy had a large number of Liberators written off in operational accidents. Judging by the chewed-up PSP in the foreground, it appears that this VB-106 PB4Y-1 suffered a violent ground loop before coming to rest in the grass 'somewhere in the South West Pacific'. In such incidents, the aircraft was usually not repaired, but was instead used as a parts source to keep the other flyers operational (*VADM John T Hayward*)

BELOW Finished in tri-colour camouflage, PB4Y-1 *Smooth Sailing* features a well-known Alberto Vargas image as its nose art. Assigned to VD-1, the Liberator had its nose modified to accept the Erco turret (*Dennis Gibbs*)

ABOVE Out over the Pacific, a tri-colour camouflaged PB4Y-1 Liberator of VD-1 heads out on a photo mission – note the cameraman in the waist position, which has its wind deflector deployed. This aircraft has also been fitted with an Erco nose turret (*Dennis Gibbs*)

LEFT After the war, the Liberator remained in Navy service far longer than it did with the USAAF. Photographed in early 1951, this interesting formation illustrates the different types flown by VC-61 just prior to the separation of the multi-engined photo-recce aircraft into VJ-61, which left VC-61 to become the Navy's first fighter photo-recce squadron. Pictured from the top right are PB4Y-1P, SNB-5, F4U-4P, F6F-5P, F8F-2P and the unit's first F9F-2P (*Ed Williams*)

ABOVE Carrying post-war national insignias, this pair of PB4Y-1s, assigned to VP-61, was photographed in July 1948 over Mt Hayes, Alaska, with the Black Rapids Glacier in the foreground. Attractively finished in overall Glossy Sea Blue, the aircraft had their tails and outer wing panels finished in red for search and rescue purposes while operating over the harsh Arctic terrain (*VADM John T Hayward*)

CHAPTER 5 | FULL METAL CANVAS

Certainly one of the most creative and carefully applied pieces of Liberator nose art was this effort painted on B-24D USAAF s/n 41-11804. Oddly, the elaborately painted aircraft does not carry a name or any form of unit marking, and may have been assigned to a Stateside unit, although it also does not appear to be with a training squadron. Also note the added windows aft of the open bomb-bay, and the 0.50-cal weapon used for defending the aircraft's belly. The Liberator carries the short-lived red surround to the national insignia

ABOVE A close-up of the right side of 41-11804 (seen on the previous page) which also affords an excellent view of the Oklahoma City Modification Center turret. Early-build B-24s, once in service, were found to be vulnerable to head-on attacks by enemy fighters, so this modification saw the replacement of the greenhouse nose with a Consolidated A-6 turret (the same as was fitted in the aircraft's tail position). The bombardier's area was also greatly modified, giving the aircraft a distinctive chin and providing more room for the crew up front

LEFT With the distinctive New York skyline in the background, *COCKTAIL HOUR* displays an attractive lass in a top hat straddling an extremely large martini. B-24L USAAF s/n 44-40428 was assigned to the Fourteenth Air Force's 425th BS/308th BG in the China-Burma-India Theatre

ABOVE With a line-up of US Navy PB4Y-2 Privateers in the background, F-7A USAAF s/n 42-73157 was assigned to the 2nd Photographic Charting Squadron at Palawan. Piloted by 1Lt Steward DeBow, and coded 2-F, *Photo Fanny's* artwork was inspired by art created by Alberto Vargas, whose stunning renditions of the feminine form graced the pages of the wartime *Esquire* magazine as well as other publications. Note the SCR-729 antennas and the braced pitot tube. By the end of the war, the unit had flown 33,000 linear miles over the Pacific on their marathon photographic mapping missions, many of which lasted for 13 hours

This excellent side view photograph of *MABEL'S LABELS* not only captures some fine, and gigantic, nose art, but also various features of the Ford-built B-24 'canvas', including a revised canopy and enlarged navigator's windows. B-24M USAAF s/n 44-50853 served with the Pacific-based 64th BS/43rd BG, and was photographed during 1945 at Ie Shima

ABOVE San Diego-built B-24J USAAF s/n 42-73327 flew with the 375th BS/308th BG, and carried the rather odd *BUZZ-Z BUGGY* nose art. Note how the navigator's small observation window has been painted over to form the 'eye' for the ferocious sharksmouth insignia

A play on words, *Liquidator* features a well-endowed blonde riding atop a martini glass while balanced on a swizzle stick! San Diego-built B-24M USAAF s/n 44-42052 operated with the 866th BS/494th BG in the Pacific. Note that this M-model does not have the characteristic enlarged navigator's window synonymous with this variant. The B-24 survived the war, but not for long, for on 10 September 1945 *Liquidator* was repatriating 20 Australian, Dutch and American PoWs when it crashed into a mountain on Formosa during a typhoon. There were no survivors

ABOVE Somebody liked cartoon characters! *IT AIN'T SO FUNNY* was Ford-built B-24L USAAF S/N 44-49853, on strength with the 64th BS/43rd BG in the Pacific. Cartoon characters included, among others, *Popeye*, *Tarzan*, *Donald Duck* and *Batwoman*. The 43rd BG was initially equipped with the B-17 Flying Fortress, but switched to Liberators between May and September 1943 while stationed at Port Moresby, New Guinea. This photograph was taken at Ie Shima in 1945

LEFT Two crewmen eagerly await a special delivery from *BOURBON BOXCAR*. F-7A USAAF s/n 42-73048 took its photos with the 20th CMS/6th PRG in the Pacific

BELOW 'Mae Wests' on, the crew of F-7A USAAF s/n 42-64047 *PATCHED UP PIECE* was photographed before a mission over the Pacific. The aircraft also flew with the 20th CMS/6th PRG. Note the extremely rough metal work under the aircraft's cockpit

ABOVE Well-dressed wolves chase a damsel in distress on the Olive Drab flank of *WOLF PACK*, which features a patch to repair flak damage just below the cockpit windscreen

RIGHT Whomever painted *PHOTO QUEEN* had a good imagination – the name was made up of photographs of nudes, girlfriends and a couple of commanding officers thrown in for good measure! F-7A USAAF s/n 42-73049 also flew with the 20th CMS/6th PRG

RIGHT Set against a Moscow skyline, *MAD RUSSIAN* was photographed at Ie Shima in 1945 – where famed war correspondent Ernie Pyle was killed by a Japanese sniper. Unfortunately, most of the artists who painted nose art did not sign their creations, and their names have been lost to time. However, this one carries the first name *Bud* just below the word *RUSSIAN*. Usually, each military base boasted one or two personnel that in civilian life had been artists or sign painters, and their talents were quickly called upon by bomber crews, who offered a few bottles of booze as payment for the artwork. *MAD RUSSIAN* was B-24M USAAF s/n 44-41846, assigned to the 65th BS/43rd BG

BELOW *"MAULIN' MALLARD"* had completed an impressive 115 sorties – recorded on the co-pilot's external armour plate – by the time the bomber was photographed upon its arrival back in the United States at Bradley Field, Connecticut, in May 1945. B-24J USAAF s/n 42-109867 flew with the 330th BS/93rd BG from Hardwick, in Norfolk. The group had flown its last combat mission on 25 April 1945 (*Lt Col Mike Moffitt*)

RIGHT Simply done *4-F* was B-24J-151-CO USAAF s/n 44-40416, which was converted into an F-7B and operated by the 4th Photographic Charting Squadron (*John A Shaw*)

BELOW *THE DRAGON AND HIS TAIL* boasted a dragon that was painted the entire length of San Diego-built B-24J USAAF s/n 44-40973, operated by the 64th BS/43rd BG. The nose art was done by motor pool mechanic S/Sgt Sarkis E Bartigall, who applied the art worn by numerous Fifth Air Force Liberators. He saw the entire aircraft as his canvas, and many crews considered him as the 'Michelangelo' of nose art

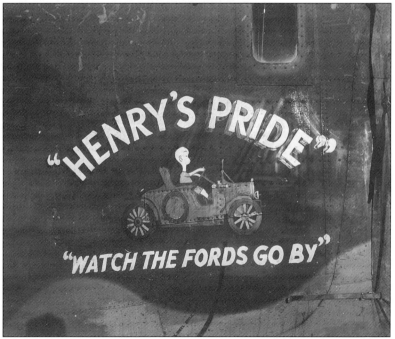

ABOVE A pleased bull eyes a lady with her clothes tangled in barbed wire on the RIP SNORTER. F-7A USAAF s/n 42-73047 flew with the 20th CMS/6th PRG

LEFT Ford-built B-24H USAAF s/n 42-7574 of the 704th BS/ 446th BG carries appropriate art and name "HENRY'S PRIDE". The 446th was nicknamed the "Bungay Buckeroos" and deployed to Britain in October-November 1943, being based at Flixton, in Suffolk (George Gosney)

LEFT B-24H-15-FO s/n 42-52705 was photographed upon its return to Bradley Field, Connecticut, in May 1945. *"TOGGLE ANNIE"* had flown with the 826th BS/484th BG from Torretto Field, in Italy. Sent to the MTO in March-April 1944 and assigned to the Fifteenth Air Force, the group's primary mission had been to bomb strategic targets in Italy, France, Germany, Rumania, Hungary, Austria and Yugoslavia (*Lt Col Mike Moffitt*)

ABOVE San Diego-built B-24J-190-CO USAAF s/n 44-41064 is seen rumbling along on a test flight near the Salton Sea in the spring of 1944, the bomber having been covered with the signatures of thousands of Consolidated employees. Numerous aircraft plants utilised 'milestone' aircraft for patriotic promotion, such as Boeing's B-17G *5 GRAND*. Often these aircraft were 'purchased' by employees who donated funds from their paychecks. It must have been a great thrill for the workers to see a gleaming bomber rolled out of the completion hangar covered with their signatures, knowing that the aircraft would soon be in action against the Axis. Consolidated's answer to the B-17G was *V GRAND*, which was the 5000th Liberator built at the San Diego factory

ABOVE The pilot of *V GRAND* forms up with another Liberator which was being used as the photo aeroplane. *V GRAND* was accepted by the USAAF on 20 June 1944 and delivered two days later. That same day, the Liberator was flown to the Combat Modification Center in Tucson, Arizona. After that, the B-24J-190-CO was transferred to Tulsa, Oklahoma, and then flown on to Mitchel Field, Long Island, where it was picked by a USAAF crew on 12 July 1944. Eleven days later the bomber flew on to Grenier and the Presque Isle, in Maine. The aircraft set out for the MTO on 31 July, and upon its arrival in Pantanella, Italy, the B-24

was initially assigned to the 783rd BS/465th BG. However, it was soon passed on to the San Giovanni-based 454th BG. The latter group had been constituted on 14 May 1943 and activated at Alamogordo, New Mexico, on 1 June 1943. The unit trained in B-24s and moved to the MTO between December 1943 and January 1944. The 454th (comprising the 736th, 737th, 738th and 739th BSs) was based at San Giovanni until July 1945. The group had initially flown tactical interdiction and support missions, bombing rail lines, marshalling yards, troop concentrations and bridges. The unit then participated in the drive

to Rome and the invasion of southern France. By then it had switched to long-range strategic missions against oil facilities, aircraft and munitions factories, harbours, airfields and industrial areas in Italy, France, Germany, Austria, Hungary, Rumania, Czechoslovakia, Albania and Greece

BELOW This was the ten-man combat crew that picked up *V GRAND* at Mitchel Field, New York, on 23 July 1944. They are, from left to right, 2Lt James Ayers (pilot), Cpl Richard Klein (gunner), Cpl Richard Keenan (gunner), Sgt Jerry Tordiglione (radio operator-gunner), Sgt Forrest Morgan (armourer-gunner), 2Lt Edward Gehrke (navigator), 2Lt Gregory Figulski (bombardier), S/Sgt James Hoard (engineer), 2Lt James Harper (co-pilot) and Cpl Perry Bailey (assistant armorer-gunner). While in service with the 454th, *V GRAND* landed twice on the Yugoslavian island of Vis, where engine changes were undertaken. Surviving its combat missions, the bomber was returned to the United States on 8 June 1945, and was noted at Cincinnati, Ohio, on 29 June 1945. The aircraft was taken over by the Air Transport Command and flown to Altus, Oklahoma, where it was turned over to the Reconstruction Finance Corporation on 26 October 1945. By 27 June 1946, some 2543 former warplanes would be parked at Altus, yet this figure represented just 7.5 per cent of the stored aircraft in the United States! Very few of these aircraft were sold to civilian buyers (fortunately, the famed B-17F *Memphis Belle* was sold and flown out, however) and by May 1948 all the aircraft had been cut up and scrapped, including *V GRAND*

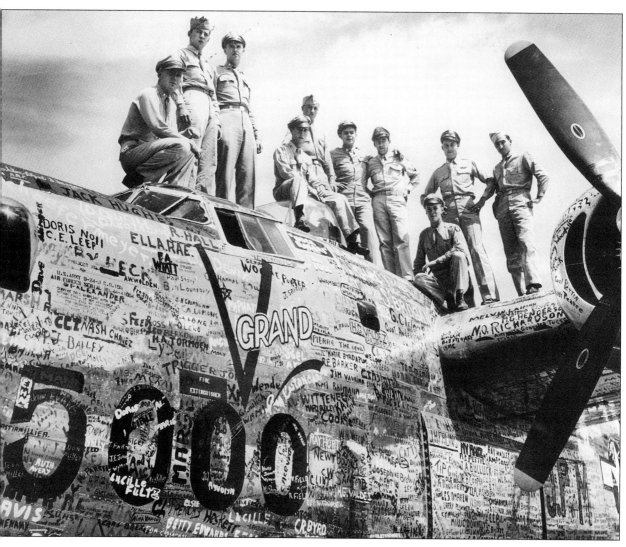

ABOVE Fort Worth-built B-24J USAAF s/n 44-44501 photographed over a heavy cloud deck. Like *V GRAND*, this aircraft's Olive Drab and Neutral Gray camouflage was covered with thousands of employee signatures although, unfortunately, the aircraft does not have a name nor any nose art. This particular B-24 was the last J-model to be built at Fort Worth under contract 40033, hence the signatures

ABOVE The crew of B-24J USAAF s/n 44-28276 *SKY'S The LIMIT* prepares to crank engines for departure from Hensley Field, Grand Prairie, Texas. Grand Prairie was home of North American Aviation's huge factory producing Mustangs and Texans. The company also took in lots of license production from other companies, and this included B-24s. North American would go on to build 430 B-24Gs and 536 B-24Js, and this particular aircraft was the very last of them

BELOW NAA employees inspect *SKY'S The LIMIT* before its departure from Hensley Field, its gleaming fresh aluminum covered with thousands of signatures. By mid 1944 Liberators were being delivered from the factories at such a prodigious rate that Combat Modification Centers could not keep up with the flow, and hundreds of brand-new bombers had to be held in storage

CHAPTER 6

THEY ALL FLEW

A relaxed crew sprawled around *THE frightful OLD PIG* – B-24J-10-CF USAAF s/n 42-84257. The aircraft was assigned to Wright Field, Ohio, for test work, and did a lot of flying with high altitude cameras. The cartoon of the inebriated pig was done by cartoonist Peter Arno, who may not have invented the single-speaker captioned cartoon, but he surely perfected it. Arno was about to abandon his ambition to be an artist for a career in music when he received a cheque for a drawing that he submitted to new humour magazine *The New Yorker* that had debuted on 21 February 1925. With the publication of this spot illustration, Arno began a 43-year association with the weekly magazine. His cartoons were particularly popular during World War 2. Note the bracing on the ungainly pitot tubes (*Lt Col Harry Trimble*)

ABOVE Its Olive Drab and Neutral Gray camouflage faded, chipped and stained, B-24J USAAF s/n 42-72994 poses with its crew during a stop over in Los Angeles while on a war bond tour. *BOLIVAR* (named after Simon Bolivar, South American general and revolutionary who led the fight to free South America from the grip of Spain – he was known as the 'Great Liberator') served with the 27th BS/30th BG in the Pacific. Note the repainting around the nose area following the installation of a new turret. *BOLIVAR's* outstanding combat record of 81 missions, 1173 hours, 186,000 miles and 405,000 lbs bombs was detailed on its lower fuselage

BOLIVAR crewmembers examine the aircraft's nose art for *12 TARGETS TO TOKYO*, which illustrates blazing islands pointing the way to Japan on America's island-hopping war in the Pacific

ABOVE With three Japanese ships, four fighters and lots of missions on its scoreboard, San Diego-built B-24D USAAF s/n 42-40323 provides a suitable backdrop for its combat-seasoned crew. This aircraft had been upgraded in-the-field with the new nose turret, and evidence of repainting around the metal work can be seen. It was not uncommon for the Liberator's huge flanks to carry more than one form or artwork, as can be seen on this aircraft, which was assigned to the 370th BS/307th BG in the Philippines in early 1945

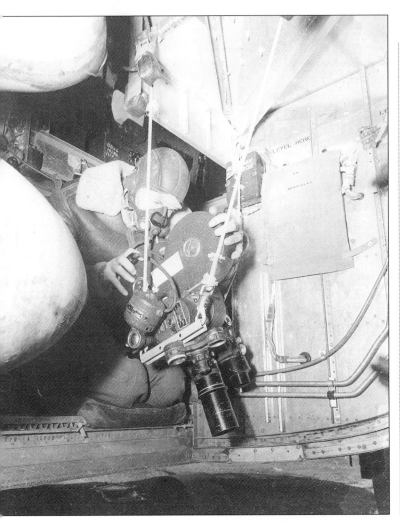

LEFT Not a particularly good place to be in a war zone! A combat cameraman practices aiming his motion picture camera through a Liberator's open bomb-bay doors. Note how bungees secure and stabilise the camera, while the cameraman himself is lashed to the structure. Bombs are to his right and the bomb-bay fuse box is above his left hand. This hazardous position was manned specifically to get film of the bombs falling on their target

BELOW The following sequence of five photographs (this page and overleaf) depict the crew of a VD-1 PB4Y-1 in and around their Liberator. In this shot, crewmen are cleaning off *THE LEMON*, which has 25 photo missions recorded. The aircraft's information block is clearly visible, identifying it as US Army B-24J-105-CO USAAF s/n 44-40346! The Navy designation and Bureau Number would have been carried on the vertical tail surfaces (*Dennis Gibbs*)

OPPOSITE LEFT *Bob's Hope* serves as an appropriate backdrop for actor Bob Hope and his very popular USO troupe. B-24J USAAF s/n 44-40395 was assigned to the 64th BS/43rd BG, based at Clark Field, in the Philippines, in the final months of the Pacific war

LEFT The pilot of *THE LEMON* hands down a maintenance form to the aeroplane's crew chief. The first Navy Liberators were simply standard Army B-24Ds that were assigned Navy Bureau Numbers. Later, Js, Ls and Ms were added, and these were all designated PB4Y-1s. Note the bulged window for extra visibility and the red-painted fire extinguisher panel (*Dennis Gibbs*)

ABOVE The youthful tail gunner of *THE LEMON* prepares to remove the canvas covers from the barrels of his 'twin fifties', fitted in his Consolidated A-6B turret. These covers prevented the weapons from suffering damage from the constant humidity and coral dust (*Dennis Gibbs*)

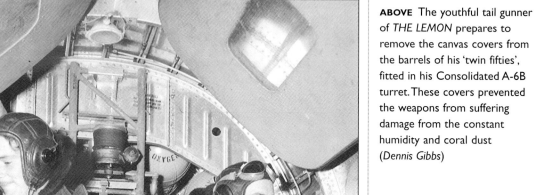

LEFT Waist gunners on *THE LEMON* prepare for a high altitude mission. Even though VD-1 was operating in the Pacific, it still got very, very cold at altitude. Of interest is how the gunners' window panels slide up and out of the way. Also note the bare metal finish to the interior (*Dennis Gibbs*)

RIGHT *THE LEMON's* nose gunner with his Engineering and Research Company (ERCO) turret. The Navy did not like the original nose armament fitted to the B-24D and numerous aircraft were retrofitted with the ERCO unit. Some of the later model Privateers were also fitted with the turret (*Dennis Gibbs*)

LEFT Given the temperatures in the Pacific, it could not have been much fun for the crew of PB4Y-1 *Slick Chick* to pose for this formal photograph. The majority of the crew are wearing their high altitude leathers, and all carry side arms. The smartest member of the 11-man crew is the aircraft commander, seen in the centre with the least amount of clothing on! *Slick Chick* was assigned to VD-5 and was operating out of Guam. Some PB4Y-1s were delivered in Olive Drab Neutral Gray camouflage but others, like this aircraft, received Navy tri-colour schemes (*Dennis Gibbs*)

LEFT Crewmen from VD-5 load cameras aboard their PB4Y-1 for an early morning mission against the Japanese. This view shows the gunner's panel to advantage, along with the retracted wind deflector. (*Dennis Gibbs*)

BELOW A sailor boresights the 0.50-cal Brownings in the ERCO turret of a VD-1 PB4Y-1. Note that the turret carries its own nose art. The incredibly worn paint scheme of this Liberator reveals a true combat veteran. Unusually, the number two engine has been shut down with its propellers feathered (*Dennis Gibbs*)

ABOVE T/Sgt Joseph Benkovic preflights his flight engineer's panel on 28 July 1942, prior to participating in an Atlantic crossing with Ferry Command. The aircraft's serial, 40-2375, is prominently carried at the top of the panel, identifying his mount as only the seventh B-24A built

ABOVE They survived to return. Battered B-24 *The Blue Streak* emerged unscathed from the deadly skies over Ploesti for a goodwill tour of the United States. Wearing dress uniforms, the crew poses with their battered bomber at Fort Worth, Texas, their visit to the Consolidated factory being a thrill for the thousands of employees involved in building new Liberators. There seems to have been little attempt made to clean up well-worn 514th BS/ 376th BG B-24D USAAF s/n 41-11613, which carries a map of the Mediterranean Theatre on the forward fuselage and RAF fin flashes on the vertical tails. The fin flash was carried by virtually all 98th and 376th BG Liberators until the autumn of 1943, this being a theatre marking for all Allied aircraft as ordered by HQ USAAF Middle East in December 1942

LEFT At another goodwill stop, the crew of *The Blue Streak* pose in less formal attire. Note the victory marks for ships and Italian and German fighters, and the way bomb missions are represented by stars on a panel. It is of interest to note that the propellers in the Fort Worth photograph are bare metal, while these are in chipped and weathered black paint, perhaps indicating a prop change somewhere along the line

ABOVE A crewman cleans off the camera port in the nose of *"Ol' Nick"*, an early-build B-24D that does not feature the cheek-mounted 0.50-cal gun adopted later in the production run. This photograph shows the three 0.50-cal nose-mounted machine guns in their K-4 sockets to advantage, however, along with the pitot tube and its protective covering. The aircraft could possibly be USAAF s/n 41-11653, which was a standard B-24D converted to XF-7 configuration at Lowry Field, Colorado, during January 1943. This aircraft was the first dedicated photo-reconnaissance variant of the Liberator, and as such had its bombing equipment removed and 11 cameras installed in aft fuselage, bomb-bay and nose positions. In July of that year, four more B-24Ds were converted into F-7s at Lockheed's facility in Dallas

LEFT After crossing the Atlantic, Ford-built B-24J-6-FO USAAF s/n 42-51451 receives a spot of maintenance from a crew chief at Bradley Field, Connecticut, on 26 May 1945. The war in Europe was over, and thousands of B-24s and other combat aircraft were ferried back to the United States for deployment or storage and scrapping. *THE CARRIER PIGEON* flew with the 564th BS/389th BG 'Sky Scorpions' from Hethel, in Norfolk, and had 36 combat mission recorded on its external armour plate (*Lt Col M Moffitt*)

BELOW Lt Stan Staples pokes his head through the sliding cockpit window of his Ford-built B-24M-6-FO USAAF s/n 44-50616, which was assigned to the Fifteenth Air Force's 461st BG at Torretto, Italy. The view shows the new, more angular, cockpit observation bubble to advantage as well as the enlarged bubble for the navigator's station. The B-24M was the last production variant of the Liberator

LEFT One for the boys. A 90th BG 'Jolly Rogers' tail serves as a backdrop for these USO lovelies during a stop over in New Guinea. Between 1942-45, the 'Jolly Rogers' lost 91 Liberators. Of this number, 25 were shot down in combat (11 of these during repeated attacks against Wewak) and a further 13 were scrapped as a result of combat damage

BELOW Wearing a wide variety of uniforms – most oil and grease stained – the crew of *American Beauty* enjoy a moment of relaxation after returning from a combat mission. This Liberator had been converted into an F-7A, and was assigned to the 6th PRG in the Pacific

CHAPTER 7

END OF THE LINE

Rather amazingly, these surplus USAAF Liberators survived at Kelly Air Force Base, Texas, into the early 1950s (*Norm Taylor*)

At the end of World War 2 the US government was left with tens of thousands of warplanes that were no longer required for active service. Storage fields were established across the United States to receive the incoming aircraft from Europe and the Pacific. However, many warplanes were scrapped on site or simply dumped off aircraft carriers at sea. Some aeroplanes, like the P-51 Mustang and A-26 Invader, were to be kept for the post-war Air Force, but the entire fleet of Liberators was declared obsolete.

The most famous of these huge storage sites was at Kingman, Arizona. During World War 2, Kingman Army Air Field was home to the Flexible Gunnery School and a Four-Engined Co-Pilot (B-17) School under the Western Flying Training Command. With the end of the war, and little use for either mission, the field was closed to USAAF operations. However, the area's excellent weather, and the large amount of acreage surrounding the base, made Kingman an ideal storage

depth for the thousands of combat aircraft returning from remote areas across the globe

The War Assets Administration (WAA) took over Kingman, and the field received a new designation – Storage Depot 41. The aircraft began pouring in – mainly Liberators and Flying Fortresses, but also hundreds of Havocs, Mitchells and Marauders, along with more esoteric types such as the Consolidated B-32 Dominator.

Today, the mind truly boggles at the number of warplanes – over 5000 combat aircraft – that eventually arrived at Kingman. The ferry crews would drop the aircraft off, jump into a transport and head back to get the next one. Of course, the main problem was what to do with this vast aerial armada. The

The Liberators at Kingman varied from factory-fresh to battle-seasoned veterans such as Ford-built B-24M-11-FO USAAF s/n 44-20728, which featured the yellow and black chequers of the Fifteenth Air Force's 758th BS/459th BG. Note how preservative had been applied to the nose area to keep moisture out of the airframe (*W T Larkins*)

ABOVE Possibly utilised for testing, this Liberator has had all of its armament removed, a tail fairing installed in place of the turret and a radome added under the modified nose. The bomber was neatly parked among several rows of B-24s at Cal-Aero, in Chino, California. The companies that formed AAC recovered 200,000,000 lbs of aluminium, 1000 ounces of platinum and 80,000 ounces of silver from the 20,000+ aircraft they scrapped. At the start of scrapping, aluminium was retailing at five cents a pound, but high civilian demand drove the price to 22 cents per pound. For an investment of $6,582,156, the partners took in $40,000,000 (*W T Larkins*)

WAA wanted to sell the aeroplanes to recoup some of the taxpayers' huge investment in the machines of war which were now unwanted, but buyers, unfortunately, were few and far between.

Initially, the task of the caring for the arriving warplanes was given to the Reconstruction Finance Corporation (RFC), since it was the only governmental immediate post-war organisation funded to advance money for the storage and sale of surplus property. Work was undertaken to preserve engines and other equipment on the arriving aircraft. Some machines were being delivered directly from aircraft production lines, while others were combat veterans featuring colourful markings and nose art. The RFC set up a pricing scale for the aircraft and parts and, as with most government operations, it was inconsistent – a whole P-38 could be purchased for $1250, but a propeller for a P-38 would cost the buyer $3800!

Buying an aircraft was simple – if the buyer had the finance, he could wander through rows of aircraft, make a selection, fill out the paperwork and become the proud owner of a former warplane at a mere fraction of its original price. Unfortunately, there were few buyers for the some 2567 Liberators parked at Kingman.

Getting rid of the aircraft was a very slow process, so the WAA started running the following advertisement on 10 June 1946, requesting bids on the aircraft stored at Kingman and the many other WAA storage depot;

'Administration will dispose of over 20,000 combat-type aircraft as scrap and salvage. These aeroplanes are observation, reconnaissance, fighters and bombers which are ineligible for certification by the CAA, and cannot be used for flight purposes. They are offered for sale as is, for the value of component parts and basic metal contents.'

Ford-built RB-24L-11-FO USAAF s/n 44-49630 was one of just a handful of Liberators fitted with a Central Fire Control system and used as a trainer for Boeing B-29 gunners (*W T Larkins*)

As the Liberators arrived, ferry crews jumped out, got into a transport and returned to pick up more aircraft. The Liberators were then towed into long rows for temporary storage. This particular Liberator was a combat veteran of the ETO, having served with the 566th BS/389th BG at Hethel (*W T Larkins*)

The bidding period closed on 1 July 1946 at the WAA headquarters in Washington DC. No bidder was allowed to get the contents of more than one field, and the winner of the Kingman storage yard was Martin Wunderlich, a construction firm from Missouri. Wunderlich Construction bid $2,780,000 for 5483 warplanes. The company had to pay ten per cent up front and follow with monthly payments. It was pretty much a giveaway price, but troubles were to follow.

In August, Wunderlich received notice that the Los Angeles WAA office was seeking bids for the gasoline and oil retained in the Kingman aeroplanes. Amazingly, there was approximately 3,000,000 gallons of fuel and oil left in the aeroplanes. Newspapers soon caught onto this boondoggle, and much publicity was generated while Wunderlich argued that their bid was for the entire aircraft, including fuel, and that the original WAA advertisements never stated anything about fuel and oil being bid separately. Wunderlich would eventually prevail, but much bad press for the scrappers and the government was generated, suggesting under the table deals to politicians.

All successful bidders, including Wunderlich, formed together to create the Aircraft Conversion Company for smelting the aeroplanes at the various fields. The government contract gave Wunderlich just 14 months to scrap the aeroplanes and clear the field. Components were rapidly removed from the aircraft – propellers were pure aluminium alloy, and melting them would cause a loss of value, so all non-aluminium parts were removed and put aside. Since there was a huge fleet of DC-3/C-47 aircraft operating post-war, R-1830 engines were removed from the Liberators and warehoused for sale – the engines moved extremely rapidly. Bicycle chain from the Liberator's control systems was purchased in bulk by a company converting push-type lawn mowers into powered units.

Since different types of aircraft had different types of alloy, they were fed into the smelters by type. As the aircraft headed to the smelters, non-aluminium materials were taken from

the aeroplane and dumped on the side. These items included instruments, life rafts, oxygen equipment and other non-aluminium goods. A crew would go through these piles, sort them out and then store them in warehouses. As the pace increased, they were melting 35 aircraft per day. No thought was giving to saving anything for historical purposes.

While all this was going on, aviation historian William T Larkins had requested, and received permission, from the WAA to visit Kingman and photograph the aircraft. Bill takes up the story;

'By the time I got there on 6 February 1947, Kingman had become a private operation. This is one of the reasons why it was so hard to get into – there was no appealing through channels to government offices. It was strictly dealing directly with a hard-headed junk dealer who was not in the least bit interested in history, or crazy aircraft collectors. It didn't take me long to find this out after driving 562 miles from San Francisco in my well-worn 1932 Model B Ford. I was told flatly that my prior request to the War Assets Administration didn't mean a thing as this was now a private operation, and they did not want people wandering about the field stealing things.

'After considerable arguing and pleading, a compromise was finally reached. If I would pay the wages of a guard to accompany me at all times, and agree to stay out of the aircraft, I would be permitted to photograph there for a day. This turned out to be a blessing in disguise, although I didn't realise it at the time, because it actually provided me with a jeep and driver for the day. The area was so large, and time so short, that if had been on my own it would have resulted in me getting fewer photos. I had the ability to simply jump out and shoot a

When the WAA auctioned off five storage facilities in 1946, the smallest was Cal-Aero Field in Chino, California. The 1340 stored aircraft were acquired by Sharp and Fellows Contracting Company for $404,593. The aircraft were reclaimed in less than a year, but fortunately Bill Larkins was able to photograph many of them, including numerous Liberators, during May 1946. Unlike Kingman, it appears that most of Cal-Aero's B-24s had been utilised in Stateside training roles like B-24D USAAF s/n 42-7341. Note how the 'last three' of the serial had been repeated on the nose. Given the fact the aircraft were to have very short lives once stored, it is rather amazing that many man-hours were expended on painting out national insignias (W T Larkins)

beautiful B-24, hop back in and charge on to the next good-looking spot.'

One must remember that aviation photographers of the immediate post-war period had a different mission than today's photographers. A group of aircraft photographers had come up with a set of rules and, since they all swapped photographs and negatives with each other, the rules had to be obeyed. Bill comments;

The first rule was complete aeroplanes, for engineless aircraft were not tolerated by collectors at that time, and I was taking a number of duplicate negatives for trading purposes. The second goal was to photograph different block numbers – again a fetish that was a result of working with James C Fahey (who published a number of guide books to military aircraft and ships), enthusiasts of that period and AAF Tech Orders. This took some extra time to do because it meant stopping, walking to the nose to read the tech data legend for the block number, and then going to another and another in search of that elusive difference. Naturally, I was interested in markings and tail letters, and attempted to get a sample of each one, but not on incomplete aeroplanes. As a result, I did not bother with large areas of B-24s and B-17s where the aeroplanes were already being disassembled.'

Everything started out well, and Bill was exposing lots of film as his guard tagged along. When it came noon, the guard insisted on a lunch hour!

ABOVE Awaiting scrapping, XB-24N USAAF s/n 44-48753 was photographed during January 1946 at Patterson Field, Ohio. Various other damaged aircraft, including a P-51H, P-47D and B-25J to the left of the XB-24, also await a similar fate (*W T Larkins*)

BELOW The story goes that the Wunderlich scrappers were so impressed by the art on this Liberator that they let the aircraft survive – temporarily. The aeroplane was pulled near the smelters and parked, and a close examination of the photograph shows the bomber's engines and other removed bits behind it (they can be seen past the nose wheel). The scrappers let *THE DRAGON AND HIS TAIL* survive as the last bomber at Kingman before feeding it into the smelter (*Peter M Bowers*)

'Can you imagine sitting in the middle of 5000+ aircraft with camera in hand and unable to do anything about it? It seemed like one o'clock would never come, but it did and we were off again for another part of the field. Since I was anxious to get as many different types as possible, it was necessary to drive over the entire area to see what was available. Readers need to realise that knowledge of the field from looking at aerial photos was not available to me at that time, and you

ABOVE Liberators and Flying Fortresses sit packed into a small storage area, their national insignia carefully painted out, but with all other combat markings left untouched. Unfortunately, the location of this storage area remains unidentified

ABOVE Fortunately, this Liberator did escape the scrappers. B-24D USAAF s/n 42-72843 emerged from its years in storage at Davis-Monthan AFB, Arizona, battered by the elements, but still intact. Put aside for eventual preservation, the Liberator was lucky, for many other stored historic aircraft parked alongside it were eventually scrapped. A veteran of the first Ploesti raid, the bomber served with the 512th BS/376th BG in the MTO, flying as the *STRAWBERRY BITCH*. In 1959 42-72843 was delivered to the USAF Museum at Wright Patterson AFB, Ohio, where it is now proudly displayed

LEFT Bill Larkins took this remarkable photograph from a low-flying Piper J-3 Cub on 8 February 1947. It shows seemingly endless rows of Liberators patiently waiting their turn to be fed into the smelter. Parked behind the B-24s are hundreds of B-17s (*W T Larkins*)

could not see past two rows of aeroplanes when you were in the middle of such a forest of machines, so when we were on the ground driving around in the jeep we really didn't know what lay ahead.'

Bill pushed on and on, and it was late afternoon when he got to the B-25s, B-26s and A-20s. A close examination of the negatives shows that camera shake was showing up on some of the shots (even at 1/400th of a second) due to the pressure of trying to get as much shooting done as possible before five o'clock.

'And of course, that doesn't mean shooting photos up to five pm. It meant driving back to the office so that the guard could check out by five pm – a considerable distance in a field that had aircraft stretching for five miles.'

Still, when it was done, Bill had compiled a significant historical record of some of the aircraft that would soon become aluminium ingots. Not completely satisfied with his one day shooting, Bill pooled what little money he had left and went literally across the street to a small civilian airport where he rented a Piper J-3 Cub.

The pilot of the Cub started by making passes at 1000 ft over Kingman while Bill clicked away from the open door. On each pass, Bill convinced the pilot to lose more and more height, until the final passes were made at about 250 ft. Today, Bill views these photographs as being historically the most valuable, since they show the scope of the entire Kingman operation.

The WAA recorded 5553 aircraft in storage at Kingman on 27 June 1946 (just 16.3 per cent of the aircraft the WAA had in storage). Today, virtually nothing remains of that vast fleet except for Bill's photographs.

CHAPTER 8

PRIVATEER

THE US NAVY had enjoyed a great deal of success with its PB4Y-1 Liberators. Much of the aircraft's work was done at lower altitudes, and when it came time to look at a replacement for these essentially surplus USAAF bombers, Navy officials got together with Consolidated to work out an optimised variant of the PB4Y-1 that was initially known as the Sea Liberator. Despite both parties hoping to use as many components as possible from the Liberator in order to keep costs down, there would be many changes incorporated into the new aircraft, which received the company designation Model 40. Work on the project began on 3 May 1943.

Since the aircraft would be operating in the lower altitudes, the powerplant chosen was the Pratt & Whitney R-1830-94 Wasp, which was not fitted with a turbosupercharger. Also, the new model engine required a different cowling and nacelle.

A decision was made to dispose of the Liberator's trademark twin tails in favour of a massive single vertical fin and rudder. This was not the only major structural change, for the fuselage was stretched seven feet forward of the wing. The Model 40 would be utilised in the battle for the Japanese Home Islands, and the Navy knew that the aircraft would be facing very heavy aerial opposition from enemy fighters. To counter this, the new aircraft was fitted with a nose turret, two top turrets, two

XPB4Y-2 BuNo 32086 was the the first of three converted PB4Y-1s, and it is seen here on a test flight from Lindbergh Field. Although having their fuselages lengthened, these aircraft initially flew with the conventional Liberator twin tails. The original single vertical tail was smaller than the unit seen in this photograph, the larger tail helping lessen the Liberator's tendency to yaw while in flight. One of the last Allied losses of the war involved Privateers on 11 August 1945, after the atomic bombs had been dropped and immediately before the unconditional surrender of Japan. Two VPB-121 Privateers were patrolling off Tokyo and Yokohama when they were attacked by enemy fighters. One aircraft was damaged and the other shot down in flames on what proved to be VPB-121's last mission of the war

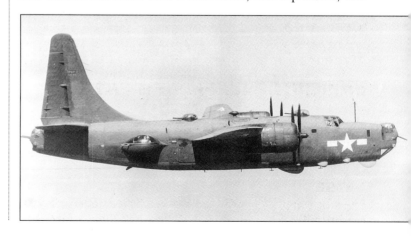

waist turrets and a tail turret for a total of 12 0.50-cal Browning M-2 machine guns.

As design work progressed, the aircraft was redesignated the Model 100, while the Navy assigned it the designation XPB4Y-2. Along with the heavy armament, the bomb-bay would be capable of lifting up to 8000 lbs of bombs. Eleven crewmembers (including two electronics operators) would be protected by 1171 lbs of armour plate, and due to the type's increased weight, provision was made for installing eight of the new Jet-Assisted Take-Off (JATO) units on the fuselage.

Three PB4Y-1s were allocated to the project, and these aircraft were suitably, but not completely, modified into XPB4Y-2s. Also, the new design had been given the suitably nautical name of Privateer. In order to speed up the process, these three aircraft were initially flown with their standard tails, but with the lengthened fuselage. The first XPB4Y-2 flew from San Diego on 20 September 1943, and a production contract for 660 aircraft was issued in October. The following year, a contract for a further 710 Privateers was issued. Let's take a look at the Privateer.

PB4Y-2 Privateer BuNo 59602 conducts a test flight off the California coast. Before the Navy switched to the overall Glossy Sea Blue camouflage scheme, Privateers were delivered in tri-colour camouflage, although many of the aircraft had a curious mottle pattern applied over the fuselage sides. During the course of 1944, Privateers were supplied to VPB-118, -119, -120, -121, -122, -123, -124 and -143. Squadrons that were either returning from combat or were converted in combat zones to Privateers included VPB-101, -102, -104, -106, -108, -109, -111, -115, -116 and -117. The training of Privateer crews was handled by VPB-197 and VPB-108

DESCRIBING THE PB4Y-2

FUSELAGE

The Privateer fuselage was a stressed skin all-metal structure which was divided into seven main compartments.

NOSE

The nose compartment of the PB4Y-2 extended from station 0.0 to station 1.0, and was equipped with a ball turret armed with two 0.50-cal guns. The bombardier's equipment and ammunition magazines for the nose turret were located within the nose compartment.

The emergency nose wheel door operation handle was located at the rear of the nose compartment at station 1.0 on the lower side of the lateral beam. A downward pull on the handle allowed the nose wheel doors to swing open for emergency exit.

FLIGHT COMPARTMENT

The forward flight compartment extended from station 1.0 to station 3.0, and could be generally described as that section of the aircraft containing the instruments and controls essential to flight. The pilot and co-pilot positions were located on the left and right sides of the forward flight compartment. Windshields were of plain double plate glass for both the pilot and co-pilot. The inner plate glass was removable. Side window blisters of plastic sheet were provided for both pilot and copilot.

NOSE WHEEL COMPARTMENT

The nose wheel compartment extended from station 1.0 to station 4.0 below the flight compartment and the radio-navigation compartment, and housed the nose wheel in its retracted position, the radio equipment, voltage regulators, reverse current relays, inverters and the aeroplane's storage batteries. A passageway was provided for access to the nose compartment, and this ran the full length of the nose wheel compartment on the right side.

RADIO-NAVIGATION COMPARTMENT

The radio-navigation compartment extended from station 3.0 to station 4.1 and housed the equipment for the radio operator, special radio operators and navigator. Located in the top of the radio-navigation compartment was the Martin top turret, with two 0.50-cal machine guns. Just aft of the top turret was the navigator's hatch, which could be used as an emergency escape exit when the aircraft was not in flight.

The navigator's hatch was equipped with a hatch cover and a transparent astrodome for celestial observations. Either of these, when not in use, could be stowed by means of straps provided at the right side of the compartment. Forward and to the left of the top turret was located an emergency escape hatch for use only when the aeroplane was not in flight.

At station 4.1 on the right side was located the fuel control panel and on the left the fuel sight gauges. A sliding door at station 4.1 and a hinged door in the deck closed off the radio-navigation compartment from the bomb-bay.

OVER-WING COMPARTMENT

The over-wing compartment extended from station 4.1 to station 5.1 over the centre section of the wing, and housed the ducts of the cabin heating and anti-icing system, as well as the radio equipment.

BOMB-BAYS

The bomb-bays extended from station 4.0 to 6.0 and were divided into four sections by a longitudinal catwalk running the full length of the bomb-bays and a reinforced transverse bulkhead at station 5.0. The four sections of the bomb-bays were referred to as the left front, right front, left rear and right rear. In each of the four sections was a bomb rack which served not only to carry bombs but as an important structural member of the aeroplane. Provision was made for the bomb-bays to be utilised to carry fuel, bombs and/or photographic equipment. The photographic equipment was installed in the right rear bomb-bay as this could be opened manually. A work table could be installed in the aft bomb-bay for photographic missions.

BOMB-BAY DOORS

The bomb-bay doors were made up of a corrugated hat section, spot-welded and riveted to an outer skin of dural. This type of construction gave sufficient strength and, at the same time, provided the flexibility required for the doors to follow a curved track over the contour of the fuselage without strain when operated. The rollers on which the doors moved were attached to each end of the hat sections. At the bottom of the sections, and on the second from the bottom corrugation, rollers were replaced by shoes which kept the tracks clear of dirt.

The bomb-bay doors were located between stations 4.0 and 6.0, and completely enclosed the lower section of the bomb-bay. The primary function of the bomb-bay doors was to provide an adequate opening in the under section of the bomb-bays for the loading and dropping of various types and sizes of bombs. The doors also provided an entrance to the aeroplane, and could be used as an emergency exit.

The doors were operated by cables attached to a crosshead on the end of a hydraulic jack. The cables ran through a pulley system and around sprockets mounted on bearings in the fuselage at each end of the doors. The sprockets engaged in the brackets to which rollers were attached and, in revolving, ran the doors up and down, utilising the rack and pinion principle. When the doors were operated hydraulically, both sides of the bomb-bays opened or closed simultaneously, but when it was desired to operate either the left or right side independently, manual operation was required.

Hand cranks, located at station 5.0 on either side of the catwalk, opened or closed the bomb-bay doors in the event of hydraulic failure, or at the discretion of the operator. To operate manually, the bomb control door selector or control valve had to be placed in the open or closed position as desired to permit the hydraulic fluid to flow into the return line, then operate the hand crank. To close doors manually, a crewman had to trip the safety latch located forward of station 5.0 in the bomb-bay. This latch prevented the doors from creeping closed.

REAR COMPARTMENT

The rear compartment was divided from the overwing compartment by a curtain at station 5.1 and from the bomb-bays by a horizontal deck between stations 5.1 and 6.0, and a bulkhead at station 6.0. In the top of the rear compartment, over the forward deck, was located a Martin turret with two 0.50-cal weapons. The propeller anti-icer fluid tank was installed at the right side of the aeroplane on the deck below the turret. Two water tanks, each of about 4.5 gallons capacity, were stored on the aft face of the bulkhead at station 6.0.

A main entrance hatch was provided between stations 7.4 and 7.6 at the bottom of the rear compartment.

An emergency escape hatch was provided at the top of the aeroplane between stations 6.0 and 6.1 for use only when the aeroplane was not in flight. Located on the right side of the aeroplane forward of the waist turret was a relief tube.

Two Erco hydraulic waist turrets of teardrop shape, each armed with two 0.50-cal weapons, were located in the rear compartment, one on either side of the aeroplane. Below the waist turrets were stowage compartments for the individual life rafts, parachutes and packs. Ammunition boxes and ammunition chutes for the waist turrets and for the rear turret were located in the floor of the rear compartment, and these could be locked from the outside with a key furnished with the aeroplane. These always had to be unlocked before take-off.

In the farthest aft section of the rear compartment was a revolving rear turret armed with two 0.50-cal machine guns.

WING

The PB4Y-2 wing was of full cantilever, stressed skin, two spar construction. It consisted of three major assemblies: centre section, right outer panel and left outer panel. The assemblies were made up of skin, front and rear spars, bulkheads and stringers. The wing was not designed to be watertight. The dihedral of the wing was fixed and non-adjustable. The outer wing panels were bolted to the centre section and not designed to fold back.

CENTRE SECTION

The centre section was continuous through the fuselage. From the aeroplane centreline, wing station 0, the centre section extended outward to wing station 13.5. The centre section of the wing consisted of five units:

1) the portion between the rear and front spar and including the spars was the interspar structure. The entire interspar area could be used as a walkway

2) the leading edge between the fuselage and the inboard engine nacelles

3) the leading edge between the inboard and outboard nacelles

4) the trailing edge which partially covered the flaps

5) the movable Fowler type flap

There were two each of units 2, 3, 4 and 5. The centre section contained the main fuel cells, the four engine nacelles, the engine mounts, wheel wells, landing lights and main landing gear. Contained in the area between the leading edge and the front spar was the heat anti-icing ducts. Aft of the rear spar and under the trailing edge were routed the flap, aileron and aileron tab cables.

OUTER PANELS

The right and left outer panels were rigidly bolted to the ends of the centre section. They consisted of five units:

1) the portion between and including the front and rear spar was the interspar area and was designed to be used as a walkway

2) the leading edge

3) the trailing edge, which partially covered the ailerons

4) the ailerons

5) the wing tips, which were designed to be removable

The outer panels contained the auxiliary fuel cells in the interspar area. The heat anti-icing ducts and electrical wiring for the formation lights in the wing tips were routed in the area between the leading edge and the front spar. Under the trailing edge was routed the aileron and aileron tab cables.

On both centre section and outer panels were numerous removable plates for access to the interior of the wing for inspection, adjustment and repair purposes.

EMPENNAGE – FIXED SURFACES

The fixed surfaces of the empennage consisted of the horizontal stabilisers, horizontal stabiliser leading edges, vertical stabiliser, vertical stabiliser leading edge, dorsal fin, dorsal fin leading edge, stub island and fairing over the tail turret. The dihedral in the tailplanes was non-adjustable.

HORIZONTAL STABILISER

The horizontal stabilisers were bolted on the sides of the stub island and were of full cantilever construction. Each stabiliser consisted of two spars, with pressed ribs or bulkhead between the spars and stringers which supported the skin between the bulkhead. The leading edge nose formers and the trailing edge formers were pressed bulkheads riveted to the front and rear bulkheads respectively. Hinge brackets for the elevators were riveted to the rear spar.

VERTICAL STABILISER

The vertical stabiliser was bolted to the top of the stub island and consisted of a front and rear bulkhead and stringers which supported the skin between the bulkheads. The leading edge consisted of bulkheads, formers and stringers. Hinge brackets were riveted to the rear spar for the support of the rudder.

OTHER EMPENNAGE ASSEMBLIES

The stub island was bolted to the top rear of the fuselage, and consisted of bulkheads and stringers. The dorsal fin was located below and forward of the vertical leading edge and was fastened to the vertical stabiliser and the fuselage. The dorsal fin leading edge was located directly forward of the dorsal fin. Its main function was to reduce the drag on the vertical stabiliser. The dorsal fin and the dorsal fin leading edge were designed only as a fairing for the vertical stabiliser.

The stub island fairing over the tail turret was made up of skin over formers, and was only to provide a smooth outline of that part of the empennage.

ARMING THE PRIVATEER

Designed for long over-water missions, the PB4Y-2 was heavily armed to defend itself against Japanese fighters while also giving the bomber more capability in attacking enemy surface targets

NOSE TURRET

The Erco 250 SH-3 (Spherical-Hydraulic) turret was located in the nose of the PB4Y-2. The turret was constructed in the shape of a sphere, with the upper portion made of Plexiglas which completely covered the gunner and all mechanical parts. The instruments necessary for the operation of the turret consisted of electrical switches, triggers and a control handle – all of which were easily accessible to the gunner.

Armour plate and bulletproof glass was installed in front of the gunner. The bulletproof glass was held in place by wing nuts and pins which were attached to lanyards. The bulletproof glass was easily removed and replaced.

The turret was gear driven. Hydraulic pressure supplied by a hydraulic motor furnished the power to actuate the turret. The motion of the turret was controlled by a control handle. A valve at the base of the control handle directed the hydraulic fluid in the proper direction so as to provide complete control in arming the guns.

The gunner's seat could be adjusted two inches vertically and horizontally. Arm rests were provided for stability in operating the control handle. Chest belts and seat belts were provided for the gunner's safety.

The armament consisted of two 0.50-cal Browning machine guns and four magazines, holding 800 rounds of ammunition. The guns were mounted on Bell adapters, type E-10, and were manually charged.

The turret could be rotated 85 degrees either side of the longitudinal centreline of the aircraft. The guns could be elevated 82 degrees above neutral and depressed 83 degrees below neutral. A number of PB4Y-2s had the Erco turret

A significant number of Privateers were delivered from the factory in tri-colour camouflage. This close up view shows the bulbous nose turret and first Martin top turret to advantage

installed with a 13-degree forward cant. This decreased the elevation from horizontal and increased the lowering of the guns by 13 degrees.

The sight was of the reflector type and was located directly in front of the gunner at eye level.

MARTIN TOP TURRETS

Two Martin top turrets were provided for the PB4Y-2. The centreline of the forward turret was located at station 3.0 and the centreline of the aft turret was located between stations 5.3 and 5.4. The turrets were Martin No 250CE-16 and 250CE-17 (Cylindrical-Electrical), the former being the forward turret and the latter the rear turret.

The upper portion of the turret (which projected above the fuselage) was encased in a Plexiglas dome. This dome allowed the gunner an unobstructed view. The turrets were so designed as to rotate continuously in azimuth (360 degrees), and to elevate the two 0.50-cal M-2 machine guns from -6.5 degrees to +85 degrees.

Both turrets were driven by electrical gear. The turret drive, actuated by 24-volt electrical units, mechanically elevated, trained and fired the weapons. The turrets were built upon turntables. These turntables consisted of an aluminium alloy casting which weighed approximately 75 lbs. This casting was machined to provide for the mounting of the two electric driving motor units (azimuth and elevation), the elevation drive torque tube, the gun cradles, the sight mounting yoke, the gunner's seat, the control unit, the supporting rollers, the armour plate, the Plexiglas enclosure, the ammunition booster unit and the fire interrupter. Integral with the casting were two hoppers, one for each gun. These hoppers collected the ejected cases and links and discharged them downward.

Profile gunfire interrupters were installed in each turret for the prime purpose of interrupting the fire of guns when they came into line with the tail structure of the Privateer.

The interrupter consisted of a cam enclosed in a protective covering. The cam was turned by the meshing of a drive pinion with the large azimuth ring gear of the turret itself. As the turret revolved, the cam was turned at the same rate. On the cam was engraved an exact duplication, in miniature, of the portions of the Privateer which could come in line with the turret guns.

Fitting onto the cam cover was a switch box containing three microswitches. The contact was opened when the switch arm button, touching the cam, struck a raised portion of the moving cam, as the turret revolved, and as the guns were raised or lowered. When this switch was opened, the gunfire immediately ceased. Fire was not resumed until the button dropped from the raised silhouette to the background level of the cam as the turret was revolved so that the outline of the PB4Y-2 was no longer in line with the guns. At the upper end of the interrupter cover was a spur gear for elevating the interrupter, as the guns were elevated. In this way, the interrupter was kept in the same relative position of elevation as the guns at all times, the interrupter moving downward as the guns were raised.

In addition to functioning as a track inside which the turret rotated, the outer ring had machined into it a circular gear. This gear mated with the pinion driven by the azimuth drive unit. The power collector ring was also attached to the outer ring. Since the outer ring assembly was stationary with respect to the aircraft, and since the drive unit was mounted on the turntable, rotation of the pinion caused rotation of the turret within the fuselage. Therefore, the complete turret, including guns, ammunition, and gunner (in fact everything except the outer ring assembly) rotated in azimuth as a unit.

The turrets were armoured with half-inch thick armour plate. This plate was attached to the forward side of the turntable. It was arranged in such a way so as to protect the mid-section of the gunner from fire within an angle of approximately 30 degrees in the direction in which the guns were pointed. The lower armour plate also supported and protected the ammunition boxes.

Each turret weighed approximately 700 lbs, complete with all equipment, but not including the gunner or ammunition.

Thirty pounds was added for each 100 rounds of ammunition, thus giving an approximate weight of 940 lbs for the turret complete with 800 rounds of ammunition.

WAIST TURRETS

The Erco 250 TH (Teardrop-Hydraulic) waist turrets were located on both sides of the PB4Y-2 between stations 6.2 and 7.3 The instruments necessary for their operation consisted of electrical switches, triggers and a control handle. All the instruments were easily accessible to the gunner.

Armour plate and bulletproof glass were installed in front of the gunner. The bulletproof glass was easily removed and replaced. The armour plate and glass swung with the guns and remained between the gunner and target at all times.

Power was brought into the turret, through electric cables, to an electric motor. This motor actuated a hydraulic pump. The pump supplied the hydraulic power which operated the turret. The desired direction of movement of the turret was obtained by operating the control handles on the Clarke control valve. Rotation of the handle grips about the column swung the guns in azimuth. Pulling the hand grips elevated the guns and pushing them depressed the guns.

Emergency hand operation was provided for both azimuth or vertical movement in case of power failure.

A foot trigger mechanism was provided, if it was necessary to use both hands to operate the turret.

The armament consisted of two 0.50-cal Browning M-2 machine guns in each turret. Four boxes, each containing 400 rounds of ammunition, were located aft of the turrets. Flexible

The side gunner was completely enclosed in the tear-shaped rear fuselage turret. Note the excellent protection provided by the the two Martin top turrets

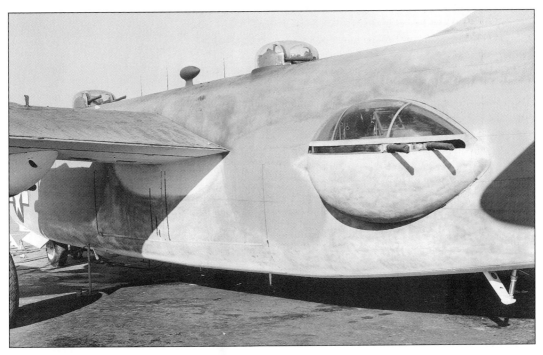

feed chutes, each of which could hold an additional 100 rounds of ammunition, conveyed the ammunition from the boxes to the guns. Thus, the supply system for each gun carried a total of 500 rounds of ammunition.

Electric boosters assisted the guns in pulling the ammunition from the boxes.

The guns in each turret could be swung 79 degrees aft, 56 degrees forward, 60 degrees up and 95 degrees down.

Fire interrupters were provided to prevent the guns from firing while they were pointed at the horizontal stabiliser and wings.

The gunner could escape from the turret by swinging the guns to their full down position. The access door was easily removed by pulling the hinge and bracket pins and by then pushing the upper section of the entrance hatch upward and outward. A parachute located near the gunner could be quickly attached to his harness.

The turret, when not in operation, was secured with the guns at 0 degree elevation and swung to the extreme rear azimuth position.

TAIL TURRET

The MPC 250-CH-6 (Cylindrical-Hydraulic) turret was located in the PB4Y-2's extreme tail position. Its function was to protect the aeroplane against attack from the rear. The turret was cylindrical. It had a Plexiglas dome over the upper rear quarter. The dome provided the gunner with unobstructed vision to the rear.

The instruments necessary for both the mechanical and manual operation of the turret were enclosed within the turret. They were all easily accessible to the gunner. The instruments consisted of electric switches, triggers and a control handle. The handle enabled the gunner to manipulate the turret at will within the operating range.

Armour plate and bulletproof glass were installed in the turret. They were mounted to the turret structure. Thus, the gunner was always protected from frontal attack. The bulletproof glass could be readily removed (in flight, if necessary) by the gunner. This could be done by pulling out the retaining pins and by then pushing outward on the glass.

The tail turret had a separate hydraulic system. This system was mounted on a panel on the right side of the aeroplane, just forward of the turret. Hydraulic power actuated the turret both in elevation and in azimuth. The Clarke hydraulic valve, which was the control valve, controlled the movements of the turret. The turret was rotated by turning the hand grips about the vertical axis. Moving the control grips fore and aft raised and lowered the guns. The control valve also controlled the speed at which the turret could be operated.

The turret could be rotated 71.5 degrees either side of the longitudinal angles of the aeroplane. The guns could be elevated 70 degrees and depressed 34 degrees from horizontal.

The armament consisted of two 0.50-cal Browning M-2 machine guns, which were rigidly mounted.

Each gun was manually charged, and 1000 rounds of ammunition were supplied for each gun. The ammunition was stowed in containers in the rear compartment of the Privateer. An electric booster assisted in pulling the ammunition from the container to the breech of the gun.

PRODUCTION

San Diego was the only plant to build the Privateer, deliveries starting in March 1944 and ceasing in October 1945 – a total of 740 were built, with the rest being cancelled as result of the end of the war. The Navy began receiving its first examples for Fleet use when VPB-118 and VPB-119 (in October 1944 the Navy combined the designations for VP patrol and VB multi-engine bombing into VPB) began converting to the type in August 1944.

On 6 January 1945 VPB-118 deployed to the Marianas to begin operations from Tinian against the Japanese. In its low-level mission, the Privateer functioned quite well, and its heavy offensive and defensive armament was of considerable use. Around 20 Privateers were modified as PB4Y-2Bs in order to

PB4Y-2 BuNo 59819 sits on the ramp at Shemya in the Aleutian Chain, Alaska, on 1 August 1945. The Privateer's four engines were particularly appreciated by crews patrolling this harsh part of the world. This view shows the completely revised cowlings to advantage. Some VPB-108 Privateers had fixed 20 mm cannon added to the nose for attacks on Japanese shipping

carry two ASM-N-2 Bat guided bombs. One Bat was mounted under each wing panel, and operators in the fuselage would utilise radar to guide the weapon to its target. Weighing 1600 lbs, and with a wing span of ten feet and a length of twelve feet, Bats were launched by a VPB-109 Privateer on 23 April 1945 against Japanese shipping in Balikpapan Harbour, Borneo. This was a historic event since it marked the first deployment of an automatic homing weapon during the war.

By VJ-Day the US Navy had 13 operational Privateer units, along with five other squadrons flying a combination of Liberators and Privateers. However, with the end of the war, the Navy did not dispose of these aircraft in as rapid a manner as the USAAF. The Navy had a distinct need for the Privateer since the aircraft offered excellent long-range performance over vast oceans. The Navy also retained numerous Liberators well after the USAAF had scrapped the majority of its once mighty B-24 fleet.

With the surprise communist invasion of Korea in late 1950, the Privateer was once again back in action – albeit in an unusual role. VP-772, VP-871 and VP-28 (these units had had their designations changed back to reflect their patrol status) Privateers were suitably modified to carry high-intensity flares to drop at night during coordinated operations with ground troops. Marine and Army personnel had the unfortunate job of attempting to make contact with the fanatical enemy, who had learned to come out only after darkness after they had been decimated by American and Allied aerial attacks in daylight.

Each Privateer could carry up to 250 flares, and a ground spotter would signal the orbiting bomber when to drop. The area

Photographed at the 1946 Cleveland National Air Races, PB4Y-2 BuNo 59640 has been fitted with eight JATO bottles for a demonstration flight. Fully armed, and camouflaged in the mottled tri-colour scheme, the aircraft has a non-standard antenna mounted directly in front of its windscreen. Post-war service for the Privateer included being used by VP-23 and VJ-2 as hurricane hunters

would be illuminated in an almost sun-like condition, and American troops, B-26 Invaders and other ground attack aircraft would hit the startled enemy. The importance of their mission was such that the Privateers were prime targets of enemy anti-aircraft fire. Carrying a variety of electronic surveillance equipment, specially modified Privateers were used for snooping flights over North Korea and China, and at least one VP-26 aircraft was shot down.

After the end of the Korean War, the Privateer soldiered on in a variety of roles – the PB4Y-2P carried cameras, the PB4Y-2M had most of the defensive equipment removed and was used for gathering meteorological data, the PB4Y-2S was optimised for anti-submarine work and other Privateers were operated by the US Coast Guard as P4Y-2Gs.

Fleet use of the P4Y-2 (designation changed in June 1951) came to an end in mid-1954, but Reserve units soldiered on for a bit longer. However, Privateers would fly on with the Navy into the early 1960s as QP-4B (originally PB4Y-2Q) target drones. These unfortunate all-red aircraft were utilised as radio-controlled targets for missiles or guns.

By now distinctly tired, the last QP-4B (call sign 'Opposite 31', named *Lucky Pierre*) was shot down near Point Mugu, California, after launching from San Nicholas Island. It was attacked by the pilot of a VX-4 A-4 Skyhawk using a Bullpup missile (an air-to-ground weapon) that was being tested to see if it could be utilised in the air-to-air role. The missile, which had been fitted with a proximity fuse, exploded over the top of the bomber, and that finished off the Navy's last Privateer!

Privateers enjoyed a long and fruitful career following the end of the war. Glossy Sea Blue P4Y-2 BuNo 66281 was assigned to Advanced Training Unit 600 when photographed. Fully armed, the aircraft has had its national insignia on the nose sprayed over with a thin coat of paint and the 'star and bars' reapplied between the wing and waist turret. Privateers were utilised for intelligence gathering missions over or near communist countries. Indeed, in April 1950 a VP-26 Privateer was shot down by Soviet MiG-15s over the Baltic Sea whilst conducting just such a mission

Naval Air Reserve Privateers stage a fighter-like break for the camera. The PB4Y was an important aircraft for the Reserves, giving the units a heavy bomber capability

The United States Coast Guard received nine Privateers which were modified into search aircraft. All turrets were removed and a bulbous framed Plexiglas nose dome was added, along with a scanner's seat. The Erco waist turrets were deleted and flat Plexiglas panels installed, as well as seats for scanners. A scanner position was also added where the tail turret had been. Designated P4Y-2G, the aircraft were attractively finished in 'aluminised' silver paint, with large yellow bands bordered in black. P4Y-2G 59688 was photographed at San Francisco Airport on 9 January 1953 (*William T Larkins*)

OTHER USERS OF THE PRIVATEER

CANADA

The Royal Canadian Air Force operated one RY-3 as 90021, which was flown by No 45 Group as an ice research vehicle. Transferred to the RCAF's Experimental and Proving Establishment, the aircraft, named the *Rockcliffe Ice Wagon,* continued to operate under the auspices of the National Research Council. Spares were difficult to come by, and some PB4Y parts were duly obtained from the Navy. Last flown in 1948, the aircraft was scrapped soon afterwards.

FRANCE

France had an urgent need for combat aircraft to fight communist aggression in French Indochina post-war. America supplied a great deal of hardware including Hellcats, Bearcats, Invaders and, initially, ten Privateers. These aircraft were P4Y-2S variants with additional anti-submarine gear, but the French removed the majority of the latter equipment and utilised the aircraft as bombers.

Based at Tan Son Nhut with *Flotille* 8F from late 1950, the aircraft were used against communist targets. Additional Privateers were supplied both as replacements and to equip a second unit, *Flotille* 24F, bringing the overall total of aircraft supplied to 24.

Following France's defeat in Indochina, Privateers went to Tunisia, where they were used in action against Algeria starting in August 1956. They also operated during the Suez crisis. The last five survivors were scrapped in the early 1960s.

HONDURAS

The economically disadvantaged Latin American nation of Honduras was the surprising recipient of three Privateers modified as transports. These aircraft found little employment, and unsuccessful attempts were made to give one of the Privateers some bombing capability.

NATIONALIST CHINA

Thirty-eight Privateers were supplied to Nationalist China between May 1952 and June 1956 for use in the country's constant fight to remain independent of mainland communist China. Some aircraft were utilised for dropping agents and intelligence gathering, and one was shot down by Burmese fighters in 1961.

PRIVATEER HAULER

As with the rest of the Liberator series, the Privateer did not escape being converted into a passenger/cargo hauler. Under the designation Model 101, Consolidated engineers modified the fuselage to carry a crew of four and 28 passengers. A cargo

the fuselage to carry a crew of four and 28 passengers. A cargo door was installed on the left rear fuselage, while a hinged nose allowed access to a cargo compartment in the extreme forward fuselage (capable of carrying 1600 lbs of freight).

Given the designation RY-3, the aircraft could, in an all-freight configuration, uplift 25,615 lbs of cargo. In March 1944 the Navy ordered 112 examples, but it appears that only 34 were delivered. Approximately 26 were delivered to the RAF, a few went to the US Marine Corps and one was retained by Consolidated. Amongst those aircraft cancelled were 63 further examples for the RAF, as well as a USAAF variant to be known as the C-87C.

Built in San Diego, the first aircraft for the RAF was delivered on 7 February 1945. Oddly known as the Liberator C IX, the aircraft went to Transport Command's No 45 Group. Mainly based in Canada, the aircraft were used by Nos 231 and 232 Sqns for long-range flights across the Pacific. After three fatal accidents, there was speculation about the type's airworthiness, and all but one of the survivors were withdrawn on 16 April 1946 and soon scrapped. As previously noted in this chapter, the sole surviving RY-3 was supplied to the RCAF, who used it as a platform for ice testing.

With the Douglas C-54 already in full production, there seemed to be little use for the RY-3, and the majority of the terminated production run was supplied to the RAF

APPENDICES

B-24 LIBERATOR SPECIFICATIONS

XB-24

Span	110 ft
Length	63 ft 9 in
Height	18 ft 8 in
Wing Area	1048 sq ft
Empty Weight	27,500 lb
Gross Weight	38,360 lb
Max Weight	46,400 lb
Fuel	2400-3000 gal
Max Speed	273 mph at 15,000 ft
Cruise Speed	186 mph
Landing Speed	90 mph
Ceiling	31,500 ft
Climb	10,000 ft in 6 minutes
Range	3000 miles with 2500 lb of ordnance
Powerplants	Pratt & Whitney R-1830-33 rated at 1200 hp each at take-off

B-24A

Span	110 ft
Length	63 ft 9 in
Height	18 ft 8 in
Wing Area	1048 sq ft
Empty Weight	30,000 lb
Gross Weight	39,350 lb
Max Weight	53,600 lb
Fuel	2150-3100 gal
Max Speed	292 mph at 15,000 ft
Cruise Speed	228 mph
Landing Speed	92 mph
Ceiling	30,500 ft
Climb	1780 fpm (initial), 10,000 ft in 5.6 minutes
Range	2200 miles with 4000 lb of ordnance
Powerplants	Pratt & Whitney R-1830-33 rated at 1200 hp each at take-off

B-24C

Span	110 ft
Length	66 ft 4 in
Height	18 ft
Wing Area	1048 sq ft
Empty Weight	32,300 lb
Gross Weight	41,000 lb
Max Weight	53,700 lb
Fuel	2364-3164 gal
Max Speed	313 mph at 25,000 ft
Cruise Speed	233 mph
Landing Speed	93 mph
Ceiling	34,000 ft
Climb	10,000 ft in 6.1 minutes
Range	2100 miles with 5000 lb of ordnance
Powerplants	Pratt & Whitney R-1830-41 rated at 1200 hp each at take-off

B-24D

Span	110 ft
Length	66 ft 4 in
Height	17 ft 11 in
Wing Area	1048 sq ft
Empty Weight	32,605 lb
Gross Weight	55,000 lb
Max Weight	60,000 lb
Fuel	2364-3664 gal
Max Speed	303 mph at 25,000 ft
Cruise Speed	200 mph
Landing Speed	95 mph
Ceiling	32,000 ft
Climb	22,000 ft in 22 minutes
Range	2300 miles with 5000 lb of ordnance
Powerplants	Pratt & Whitney R-1830-43 rated at 1200 hp each at take-off

B-24H

Span	110 ft
Length	67 ft 2 in
Height	18 ft
Wing Area	1048 sq ft
Empty Weight	36,500 lb
Gross Weight	56,000 lb
Max Weight	65,000 lb
Fuel	2364-3614 gal
Max Speed	296 mph at 25,000 ft
	300 mph at 30,000 ft
Landing Speed	95 mph
Ceiling	30,000 ft
Climb	20,000 ft in 25 minutes
Range	2100 miles with 5000 lb of ordnance
Powerplants	Pratt & Whitney R-1830-65 rated at 1200 hp each at take-off

XB-24N

Span	110 ft
Length	67 ft 2 in
Height	26 ft 9 in
Wing Area	1048 sq ft
Span	110 ft
Length	67 ft 2 in
Height	26 ft 9 in
Wing Area	1048 sq ft
Empty Weight	38,300 lb
Gross Weight	56,000 lb
Max Weight	65,000 lb
Fuel	2814-3614 gal
Max Speed	294 mph at 30,000 ft
Cruise Speed	213 mph
Landing Speed	95 mph
Ceiling	28,000 ft
Climb	20,000 ft in 29 minutes
Range	2000 miles with 5000 lb
Powerplants	Pratt & Whitney R-1830-75 rated at 1350 hp each at take-off

PB4Y-2

Span	110 ft
Length	74 ft 7 in
Height	29 ft 2 in
Wing Area	1048 sq ft
Empty Weight	37,405 lb
Gross Weight	64,000 lb
Fuel	2364-3964 gal
Max Speed	247 mph at 14,000 ft
	238 mph at sea level
Cruise Speed	158 mph
Landing Speed	96 mph
Ceiling	19,500 ft
Climb	990 fpm (initial)
Range	2630 miles with 4000 lb of ordnance
Powerplant	Pratt & Whitney R-1830-94 rated at 1350 hp each at take-off

LIBERATOR SERIALS

CONSOLIDATED PRODUCTION SAN DIEGO

TYPE	SERIAL
XB-24	39-556
YB-24	40-702
LB-30A	AM258 to AM263
LB-30B	AM910 to AM929
B-24A	40-2369 to -2377
LB-30	AL503 to AL641
B-24C	40-2378 to -2386
B-24D	40-696 to -701, 40-2349 to -2368, 41-1087 to -1142, 41-11587 to -11938, 41-23640 to -24339, 42-40058 to -41257 and 42-72765 to -72963
B-24J	42-72964 to -73514, 42-99936 to -100435, 42-109789 to -110188 and 44-40049 to 41389
B-24L	44-41390 to -41806
B-24M	44-41807 to -42722

SAN DIEGO TOTAL – 7645

CONSOLIDATED FORT WORTH

B-24D	41-11588 to -11705 and 41-63725 to -64046
B-24E	41-29009 to -29115 and 42-64395 to -64431
B-24H	42-64432 to -64501, 41-29116 to -29608 and 42-50277 to -50451
B-24J	42-64047 to -64394, 42-99736 to -99935, 44-10253 to -10752, 42-50452 to -50508 and 44-44049 to -44501
AT-22	42-10726, 43-30549, 43-30561, 43-30574 and 43-30584
C-87	Various conversions with 42-107249 to -107275, 43-30548 to -30627, 44-39198 to -39298 and 44-52978 to -52987
C-87A	Various conversions

FORT WORTH TOTAL – 3034

DOUGLAS TULSA

B-24D	41-11754 to -11756, 41-11864, 41-23725 to -23727 and 41-23756 to -23758
B-24E	41-28409 to -28573 and 41-29007 and -29008
B-24H	41-28574 to -29006 and 42-51077 to -51225
B-24J	42-51226 to -51430

TULSA TOTAL – 964

FORD WILLOW RUN

B-24E	42-6976 to -7464 and 42-7770
B-24H	42-7465 to -7769, 42-52077 to -52776 and 42-94729 to -95503
B-24J	42-95504 to -95628, 42-50509 to -51076, 42-51431 to -52076 and 44-48754 to -49001
B-24L	44-49002 to -50251
XB-24N	44-48753
B-24M	44-50252 to -51928
YB-24N	44-52053 to -52059

WILLOW RUN TOTAL – 6792

NORTH AMERICAN DALLAS

B-24G	42-78045 to -78474
B-24J	42-78475 to -78794 and 44-28061 to -28276

DALLAS TOTAL – 966

GRAND TOTAL: 19,401

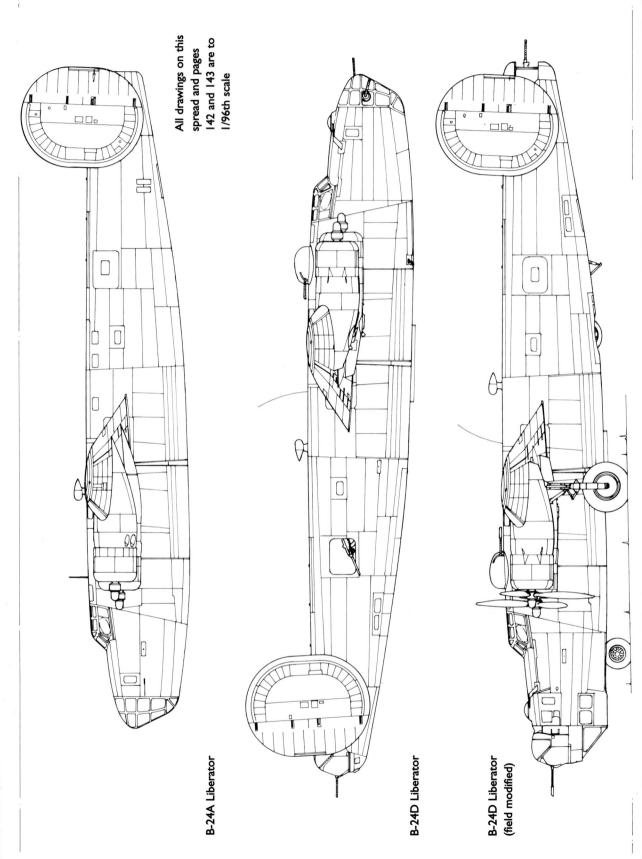

All drawings on this spread and pages 142 and 143 are to 1/96th scale

B-24A Liberator

B-24D Liberator

B-24D Liberator
(field modified)

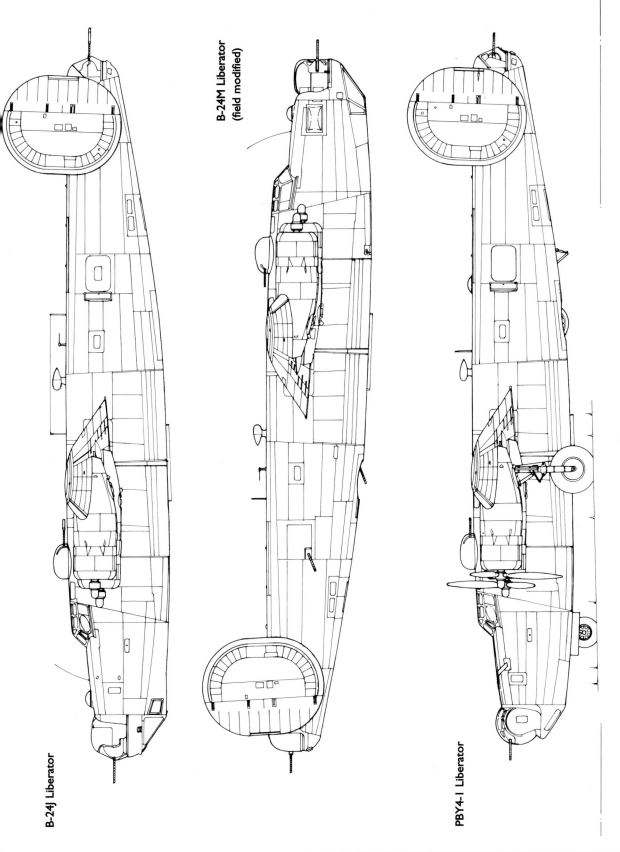

B-24J Liberator

B-24M Liberator
(field modified)

PBY4-1 Liberator

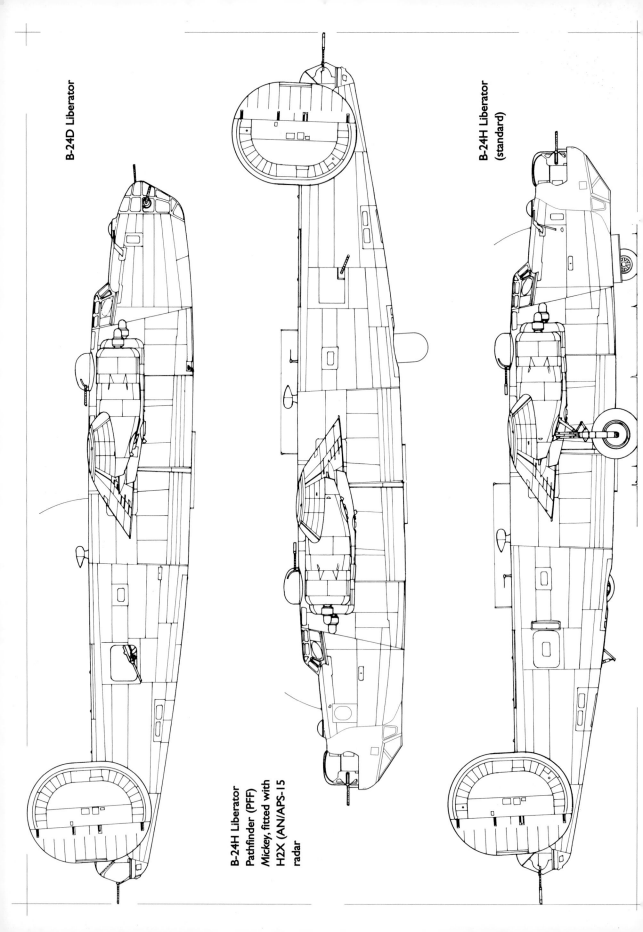

B-24D Liberator

B-24H Liberator (standard)

B-24H Liberator
Pathfinder (PFF)
Mickey, fitted with
H2X (AN/APS-15
radar

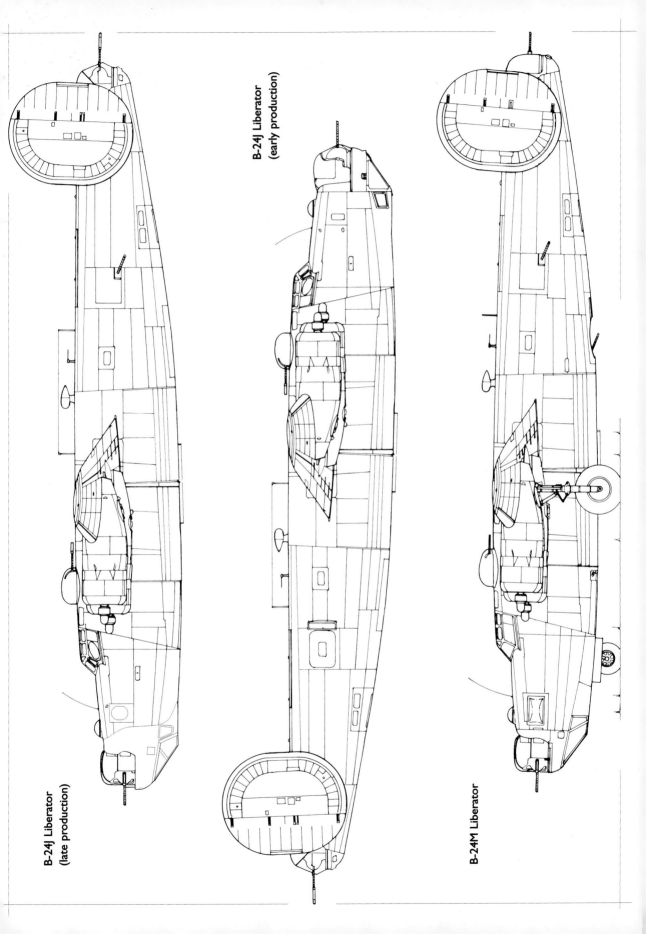

B-24J Liberator
(late production)

B-24J Liberator
(early production)

B-24M Liberator

INDEX

References to illustrations are shown in **bold**.